W9-AVL-416

THE STORY OF

Baseball

LAWRENCE S. RITTER

FOREWORD BY TED WILLIAMS

THIRD REVISED AND EXPANDED EDITION

A BEECH TREE PAPERBACK BOOK
New York

For Julio, Benjamin, and Julia with love

Text copyright © 1983, 1990, 1999 by Lawrence S. Ritter

All rights reserved. No part of this book may be reproduced or
utilized in any form or by any means, electronic or mechanical,
including photocopying, recording, or by any information storage
and retrieval system, without permission in writing from the
Publisher. Previous editions published in 1983 and 1990 by
William Morrow and Company. Revised and expanded edition
issued in hardcover by Morrow Junior Books in 1999. Published
by arrangement with the author. Inquiries should be addressed to
William Morrow and Company, Inc., 1350 Avenue of the Americas,
New York, NY 10019.
www.williammorrow.com

Printed in the United States of America

The Library of Congress has catalogued the Morrow Junior Books
edition of The Story of Baseball as follows:
Ritter, Lawrence S.
The story of baseball/by Lawrence S. Ritter; foreword by Ted
Williams.—Rev. and expanded ed.
p. cm.
Includes index.
Summary: Traces the history of baseball, which was first played
in a form resembling the modern game in Hoboken, New Jersey,
in 1846, and first played by professional players in 1869.
ISBN 0-688-16264-9
1. Baseball—United States—History—Juvenile literature.
[1. Baseball—History.] I. Title.
GV863.A1R57 1999   796.357'0973—dc21   98-35456   CIP AC

10 9 8 7 6 5 4 3 2 1
First Beech Tree Edition, 1999
ISBN 0-688-16265-7

*F*OR A LONG TIME, I'VE BEEN LOOKING FOR A GOOD BOOK
that explains the fundamentals of baseball to youngsters and intro-
duces them to the great players of the past. Now I don't have to look
any further, because Larry Ritter has come up with exactly what I've
always wanted. *The Story of Baseball* is the perfect introduction to what
baseball is all about.

You can't fully appreciate today's players unless you also know
about the great stars who preceded them. When I was growing up in
San Diego in the 1920s and early 1930s, Babe Ruth was the biggest
name in baseball. Reading about him—and about others, too, like Ty
Cobb and Rogers Hornsby and Bill Terry—inspired me to try to be
as good as they were. Looking back on it now, I don't think I ever felt
as though I was just playing against nine men on an opposing team.
I always had Ruth and Cobb and Hornsby and Terry way in the back
of my mind. I think I was always trying to surpass them in the record
books as much as I was trying to win that day's ballgame.

Tradition means a lot in baseball, which is one reason the game
plays such a special role in American life. Babe Ruth, Lou Gehrig, and
Jackie Robinson, for example, aren't only a part of baseball's past;
they are an important part of America's history, too.

Just about all of Babe Ruth's records have been broken by now, but
people still argue about whether Hank Aaron was a better home run
hitter than the Babe. Just as they debate whether Walter Johnson was
really the greatest pitcher of all time, and whether they would rather
have Tris Speaker, Joe DiMaggio, or Willie Mays as their center fielder.
Of course, there aren't any conclusive answers to such questions. But

after you've finished *The Story of Baseball*, you'll at least have the background you need to form an intelligent opinion on these issues and on many others as well.

The chapters on hitting, pitching, fielding, and managing are the most interesting introductions to these subjects I've ever seen. This is a fun book. It is also informative, entertaining, and unique. Larry Ritter says he wrote it for youngsters, but whether you're eight or eighty, I think you'll love it. I know I did.

Ted Williams

CONTENTS

part *One*

Opening Day, April 29, 1886, at the old Polo Grounds on Fifth Avenue and 110th Street in New York City. New York is playing Boston.

*B*ASEBALL HAS BEEN PROVIDING US WITH FUN AND excitement for more than a hundred and fifty years. The first game resembling baseball as we know it today was played in Hoboken, New Jersey, on June 19, 1846. The New York Nine beat the New York Knickerbockers that day, 23–1.

The game was played according to rules drawn up by Alexander J. Cartwright, a surveyor and amateur athlete. It is a myth that Abner Doubleday invented baseball. It was Alexander Cartwright, not Abner Doubleday, who first laid out the present dimensions of the playing field and established the basic rules of the game.

The first *professional* baseball team was the Cincinnati Red Stockings, who toured the country in 1869 and didn't lose a game all year. Baseball began to attract so many fans that in 1876 the National League was organized—the same National League that still exists today.

Although the game as it was played in 1876 was recognizable as baseball—nobody would confuse it with football or basketball—it was quite a bit different from baseball as we know it now. For example, pitchers had to throw underhand, the way they still do in softball; the batter could request the pitcher to throw a "high" or "low" pitch; it took nine balls, rather than four, for a batter to get a base on balls; and the pitching distance was only forty-five feet to home plate.

The rules were gradually changed over the following twenty years, until by about 1900 the game was more or less the same as it is today. In 1884, pitchers were permitted to throw overhand; in 1887,

9

the batter was no longer allowed to request a "high" or "low" pitch; by 1889, it took only four balls for a batter to get a base on balls; and, in 1893, the pitching distance was lengthened to the present sixty feet, six inches.

Players didn't start to wear gloves on the field until the 1880s. At first, they wore only a thin piece of leather over the palm of the hand, with five holes cut out for the fingers to go through. By the 1890s, however, the gloves began to look like today's baseball gloves, although they were not nearly as large.

Gloves remained more or less the same from around 1900 to the mid-1950s. The ball was caught in the "pocket" of the glove, covering the palm of the hand, and it was held with the fingers. The fingers of the glove were short and fairly flexible. The only purpose of the glove was to protect the palm and fingers from injury, although until the 1930s many players insisted on cutting a rather large hole in the palm of the glove in order to grip the ball better.

Nowadays, the glove is much larger than it used to be, and the ball is not caught in the palm of the hand but trapped in the glove's webbing, between the thumb and forefinger. Since the mid-1950s, the glove has become more of a net with which to snare the ball rather than just a protective covering for the hand.

The baseball fields were nowhere near as well taken care of as they are now, so that it was not at all unusual in the old days for the ball to take bad bounces because of pebbles in the infield or uneven ground in the outfield.

Sometimes the ball took a crazy bounce because it was a little lopsided. Since only two or three baseballs would be used for a whole game, by the seventh or eighth inning the ball was often in pretty bad shape. Indeed, this was true until the 1920s. If a ball, like a foul ball or a home run, went into the stands, the ushers would try to get it back, sometimes offering whoever had it a free pass to another game. If they succeeded in getting it back, it would be returned to the field, and the game would continue with the same ball. Now, of course, close to a hundred baseballs are used in an average big league game.

Until the early 1900s, one umpire took care of the entire field. Typically, he would call balls and strikes from behind the catcher until a man got on base, and then move out and call balls and strikes from behind the pitcher so he could be closer to the bases in case of an attempted steal.

With only one umpire, there was plenty of opportunity for mischief. A favorite trick was pulled by a man who was on second base, with the umpire working from behind the pitcher. If the batter got a hit to right field, the umpire would have to watch the ball and possibly the batter rounding first base and trying for second. Meanwhile, the man who had been on second base would take off toward home before he got as far as third, never coming anywhere close to third base.

Tim Hurst, a famous umpire in the 1890s who knew all the tricks of the trade, once called a player out who slid across home plate in a cloud of dust even though no one was even trying to tag him. Tim had been looking toward right field and second base all the while, but then he whirled around and yelled, "You're out!"

"What do you mean I'm out?" the player screamed. "They didn't even make a play on me."

"You never touched third base," Tim shouted back.

"Of course I did," the player responded. "And anyway, how do you know? You weren't even watching."

"That's just it," the umpire said. "For when I wasn't watching, you got home too fast!"

Needless to say, Tim Hurst won the argument, as have almost all umpires before and since.

In 1901, a second major league, the American League, was established alongside the twenty-five-year-old National League. Many of the stars of the National League jumped over to the new American League because they were offered higher salaries. Ballplayers didn't make the kind of money in those days that they make now, of course, but even then dollars and cents played an important role in professional baseball.

After some initial hard feelings, the pennant winners of the two major leagues met each other in 1903 in the first modern World Series. The stage was set for a great and long-lasting rivalry, one that continues to this very day.

MATTY, HONUS, TY, AND WALTER

*M*ODERN BASEBALL DATES FROM ABOUT 1900. THE four greatest players in the early years—from 1900 to 1920—were Christy Mathewson, Honus Wagner, Ty Cobb, and Walter Johnson. Christy Mathewson and Walter Johnson were pitchers, Honus Wagner was a shortstop, and Ty Cobb was an outfielder.

Everyone agrees that in general athletes are better today than they were many years ago. They are bigger, stronger, and faster. Even so, everyone who saw them also agrees that if Matty, Honus, Ty, and Walter could somehow magically return today, they would be as great now as they were then.

Although the rules of the game haven't changed much since 1900, something else has: At that time, ballplayers were looked down upon by the general public. They were considered uneducated roughnecks, not good enough to associate with respectable people. They were treated like second-class citizens.

Many years later, Sam Crawford, a great outfielder with the Detroit Tigers in the early 1900s, told a friend what it used to be like then. "Baseball players weren't too much accepted in those days," he said. "In fact, we were considered to be pretty crude. When we traveled to play in other cities, for example, they wouldn't let us in the best hotels most of the time. And when we did manage to get into a good hotel, they wouldn't boast about having us. Like if we went into the hotel dining room, they'd shove us way in the back so we wouldn't be too conspicuous."

Sam thought for a moment and then laughed. "I remember when I was with the Detroit team in 1903, one evening we all went into the dining room of this fancy hotel in St. Louis. The dining room had a tile floor made out of little square tiles. We sat there—way in the back, as usual—for about twenty minutes and couldn't get any waiters. They wouldn't pay any attention to us. Well, finally, our shortstop said he knew how we could get a waiter. And I'll be darned if he didn't take one of the plates off the table and toss it way up in the air. When it came down on that tile floor, it smashed into a million pieces. Sure enough, we had four or five waiters around there in no time."

Christy Mathewson in 1901

The public's opinion of ballplayers as rowdies, roughnecks, and punks disappeared between 1905 and 1910 due in large part to the efforts of three men.

They were John J. McGraw, the fiery manager of the New York Giants; Connie Mack (his real name was Cornelius McGillicuddy), the kindly manager of the Philadelphia Athletics; and Christy Mathewson, the greatest pitcher of his day.

Managers John McGraw and Connie Mack insisted that their players act like gentlemen and dress in suits and ties when they were off the field. Once they had accomplished this, they repeatedly asked the best hotels and restaurants to accept their teams. Eventually, they succeeded in gaining admittance just about everywhere.

Matty warming up

Christy Mathewson helped change the public's attitude toward ballplayers by the example he set, always conducting himself with dignity and respect for others both on and off the field. He was so idolized throughout the country that people started thinking that if he was a baseball player, then baseball players must be okay.

Christy Mathewson was born in 1880 in Factoryville, Pennsylvania. He went to Bucknell University, where he played football as well as baseball. He was also an honor student and a member of the glee club and the college literary society. Handsome, modest, a superb athlete, he was the original all-American boy, and by his behavior and his pitching he became the idol of millions.

Matty's pitching feats are legendary. Thirteen times he won twenty or more games, and in four of those seasons he won thirty or more.

In 1905, he won thirty-one games and lost only eight, and in 1908 he won thirty-seven and lost only eleven. He was untouchable in the 1905 World Series, winning three games in the space of six days and not allowing a single run in any of them. Over his career, which stretched from 1900 to 1916, almost all with the New York Giants, he won a total of 373 games.

He achieved his success against opposing batters with a fastball, a sharp-breaking curve, and a reverse curve that he called his "fade-away." Mathewson was a right-handed pitcher, and an ordinary curve thrown by a right-handed pitcher curves *away from* a right-handed batter. But Matty's reverse curve, or fadeaway, curved in *toward* a right-handed batter, not away from him. Today such a pitch would be called a screwball.

For many years, Mathewson's catcher was Chief John Tortes Meyers, a Cahuilla Indian from Southern California, who was the Giants' regular catcher from 1909 to 1915. Years later, when he was over eighty years old, Chief Meyers recalled what Matty was like in those days:

> "How we loved to play for that guy! We'd break our necks for him. If you made an error behind him, or anything of that sort, he'd never get mad or sulk. He'd come over and pat you on the back. He had the sweetest, most gentle nature. Did you know that he was a great checkers player, too? He was checkers champion of half a dozen states. He'd play checkers with ten or twelve opponents all at once and beat every one of them. Actually, that's what made him such a great pitcher—his wonderful retentive memory combined with his great control. Anytime someone hit a ball hard off of him, you can bet that fellow never got another pitch in the same spot again."

One of Mathewson's toughest opponents—not in checkers but in the batter's box—was Honus Wagner, the hard-hitting shortstop for the

Pittsburgh Pirates. There has never been a shortstop, before or since, who could hit like Wagner.

Most shortstops are noted more for their fielding than for their hitting. But Wagner's batting average was .300 or better for *seventeen* consecutive seasons, and he led the National League in batting a record eight times (a record recently tied by Tony Gwynn). If you are not an expert on batting averages, the chapter on batting in Part Two discusses what batting averages mean and how to calculate them.

If Honus Wagner didn't hit like a typical shortstop, he didn't look like one, either. Most shortstops are slim and graceful. Not Honus. He was built more like a weight lifter. A bit under six feet tall, he weighed a solid two hundred pounds and was as bowlegged as a cowboy who has spent all his life on horseback. Nevertheless, he was remarkably fast for a big man, as shown by the 722 bases he stole in his career.

Honus didn't glide around the infield like a greyhound, making hard plays look easy. Quite the opposite. He looked more like a grizzly bear, scrambling after any ball hit in his direction, scooping it up with his huge hands, along with any dirt that happened to get in the way, and firing the whole thing over to first base—dirt and all. It didn't look too smooth or graceful, but it must have been effective, because most experts consider him the greatest all-around shortstop who ever lived.

Wagner was a more sociable person than Mathewson. While Matty was reserved and shy, especially with people he didn't know, Honus was friendly and talkative. He was always ready to stop and chat, even with strangers. This made him extremely popular with the fans not only in Pittsburgh—where he was born and played most of his career—but in every other city around the league as well.

One thing Honus did *not* like, however, was cigarettes. In those days, baseball cards often came with packs of cigarettes. In 1909, without his knowledge, a cigarette company issued a Honus Wagner card with his picture on the front and the name of the brand of

Honus Wagner in 1908

cigarettes on the back. Honus refused to be associated with cigarettes in any way. As soon as he found out about it, he demanded that all the cards that were still in the stores be withdrawn and destroyed.

As a result, only a few are known to exist today. Because they are so rare, collectors of old baseball cards now value them at many thousands of dollars each. To be precise, in 1996, a 1909 Honus Wagner card in perfect condition was sold for $667,000!

After his great playing career ended in 1917, Honus became a coach with the Pirates, a position he held until he retired in 1951 at the age of seventy-seven. As he grew older, he enjoyed telling stories about his playing days, many of which are hard to believe, to say the least.

One of his favorites was about when he was called on to pinch-hit one day with the score tied in the bottom half of the ninth inning. "I hit a home run," Honus would say, "but I was so excited that I ran around the bases the wrong way, starting at third base, and when I crossed home plate, they subtracted a run, and we lost the game!"

Another was about the time he was reaching for a ground ball and instead of the ball grabbed a rabbit that had just run onto the field.

"I threw the rabbit to first base," said Honus, "and got the runner by a hare!"

Although Wagner hit .300 or better for seventeen consecutive years and led the National League in batting eight times, he was not the greatest hitter of his time. That honor goes to Tyrus Raymond Cobb, who was the greatest hitter of *all* time.

Ty Cobb hit over .300 for an amazing twenty-three consecutive years, spanning the period from 1906 through 1928. In three of those years, he did something only seven others have accomplished since 1900—he hit over .400. His batting average was .420 in 1911, .410 in 1912, and .401 in 1922.

He led the American League in batting a record twelve times, and his lifetime batting average was a phenomenal .367. No one else has ever come close to that figure. (Honus Wagner's lifetime batting average was .329.) Cobb also held the record for most lifetime hits—4,191—until Pete Rose surpassed him in 1985 by getting his 4,192nd hit.

Ty Cobb was born in a small town in Georgia in 1886. He threw right-handed but batted left-handed. He held his hands a few inches apart on the bat and learned to bunt or slap line-drive hits precisely where he wanted them. He made place hitting an art.

After a couple of seasons in the minor leagues, he joined the Detroit Tigers as an outfielder in August 1905, four months short of his nineteenth birthday. Two years later, he hit .350 and led the American League in batting average, hits, runs batted in, and stolen bases.

From then on, the "Georgia Peach" only improved with time. In 1927, at the age of forty, he was still able to hit .357 and steal twenty-two bases.

Many years later a youngster asked Lefty O'Doul, who also had been a great hitter, what he thought Ty Cobb would hit now, playing under present-day conditions.

"Oh, I'd say he'd hit about .330 or so," O'Doul replied.

"Then why do you say Cobb was so great?" the youngster asked. "After all, there are half a dozen players around who can hit .330."

"Well," O'Doul answered, "you have to take into consideration the man would now be eighty years old!"

Cobb was particularly dangerous in the late innings of a close game because he was always a threat to break it open singlehandedly. Not with a home run, because that wasn't his style. Instead, he did it with speed, cleverness, deception, and intimidation.

His specialty was a perfectly placed bunt to get on first base . . . soon he would be taking a long lead off the base to distract the pitcher . . . a sudden dash for second, spikes flying, and a fallaway slide to avoid the second baseman's tag . . . sprinting to third base on a wild pickoff attempt by a nervous pitcher . . . and then, amid mounting tension, the final climax . . . a false start . . . another false start . . . and a blur on the base path, a cloud of dust, and a spikes-high slide over home plate.

Ty Cobb successfully stole home a record fifty times!

He stole ninety-six bases in 1915, which remained the single-season record for stolen bases until 1962. Over his entire career, he stole 892 bases, which was the lifetime record for stolen bases for fifty years, until it was surpassed by Lou Brock in 1977.

Ty Cobb was the greatest and most exciting player of his generation, perhaps of all time. Unfortunately, he was also the most *disliked* player of his generation, perhaps of all time.

From all reports, he was mean, selfish, arrogant, and bigoted. His fierce determination to be number one, to win no matter what it cost, left little room for kindness, compassion, or friendship.

Davy Jones played in the Detroit outfield next to Cobb for many years. In an interview with a reporter years later, he talked about Ty's personality.

"The trouble was," he said, "Cobb had such a rotten disposition it was hard to be his friend. He antagonized so many people hardly

Ty Cobb

anyone would speak to him, even among his own teammates. Ty didn't have a sense of humor. Especially, he could never laugh at himself. Consequently, he took a lot of things the wrong way. What usually would be an innocent wisecrack would start a fistfight if Ty was involved. It was too bad. He was one of the greatest players who ever lived, and yet he had so few friends. I always felt sorry for him."

In his older years, Cobb mellowed somewhat. But it was too late. When he died, in 1961, only three men from all of major league baseball attended his funeral.

Ty Cobb sliding into third. The year is 1910, and the third baseman is Jimmy Austin.

* * *

In terms of personality, the modest Walter Johnson was another story altogether. Born in Kansas in 1887, he joined the Washington Senators in the American League in 1907. He remained there for twenty years, never pitching for anyone else. He hit his stride in 1910 when he won twenty-five games for a next-to-last-place team. He won twenty or more games a dozen times, including more than thirty in both 1912 and 1913.

Walter rarely pitched with a decent team behind him. In those days, a popular joke was that Washington was first in war, first in peace, and last in the American League. Even with such poor support, Walter Johnson is the *all-time leader in games won in the twentieth century*, with 416 victories—forty-three more than Christy Mathewson. (The legendary Cy Young won over five hundred games, but he won most of them before 1900.)

Walter is also the all-time leader in shutouts, with 110. Actually, the Washington team scored so few runs that he often *had* to pitch a shutout to win.

He won most of those 416 games with just one kind of pitch—a jet-propelled fastball. Late in his career, he developed a curve, but it was never very good. It didn't matter, though, because his fastball was enough. The batters knew what was coming, but they still couldn't hit it. Often, they said, they couldn't even see it.

One of baseball's classic stories takes place on an overcast September afternoon when Walter Johnson and his catcher decided to try an experiment. It was said so often that Walter's pitches were too fast to see that they decided to find out what would happen if a pitch *really* couldn't be seen.

Conditions were perfect for the experiment. It was late in the afternoon, with darkness starting to fall, so that it was hard to see the ball, anyway. And it was the bottom half of the ninth inning, with two outs and two strikes on the batter. One more strike and the game would be over.

The catcher walked out to the pitcher's mound for a conference with Johnson, and when he returned to his position behind home plate, he had the ball with him—concealed in his big catcher's mitt.

Walter Johnson stepped on the mound, wound up, and went through his complete pitching motion. An instant after he apparently threw the ball, the catcher smacked it loudly into the center of his mitt and then moved his bare hand away so that the ball was plainly visible.

"Strike three!" the umpire shouted with just a moment's hesitation. Mumbling to himself, the batter turned toward his dugout, and so ended the ball game.

Was Walter Johnson the fastest pitcher who ever lived? Old-timers swear he was and speak of his speed with awe. Others say that Lefty Grove or Bob Feller or Sandy Koufax or Nolan Ryan was even faster.

There is no way to really settle the argument, but what is certain is that Walter Johnson led the league in strikeouts twelve times and over his entire career struck out a total of 3,508 opponents. For fifty-five years that was the lifetime strikeout record, until it was surpassed by Nolan Ryan in 1983, when Nolan fanned his 3,509th batter

Humble, generous, good-natured, Walter always worried that he might injure a batter with his fastball. Regardless of the provocation, he would never deliberately throw at anyone. Like Honus Wagner, he was popular with players and fans throughout the league. Indeed, near the end of his career, most fans seemed to think it was a privilege just to see him pitch regardless of whether their team won or lost.

In 1936, nine years after he had stopped pitching, Walter Johnson came out of retirement to make one more historic throw. He agreed to try to duplicate George Washington's celebrated feat of throwing a silver dollar across the Rappahannock River at Fredericksburg, Virginia. Standing on the riverbank, his shoes in the mud, Johnson wound up and was short with his first attempt. He wound up again, and this time made it with plenty to spare.

The length of his throw was estimated at 317 feet. With characteristic modesty, he said, "I guess the river must be narrower than in George Washington's time."

Walter Johnson
in 1908

Walter Johnson, left, and teammate Clyde Milan. The year is 1913, when Walter won thirty-six games and lost only seven, and Milan hit .301 and stole seventy-five bases.

• • •

By the early 1900s, the rules of the game had evolved into just about what they are now. However, although the rules were about the same as now, the way the game was actually played was something else again.

The game was played differently then simply because the ball was different. It *looked* just like today's baseball, but when it was hit, no matter how hard, it did not carry long distances. Balls were hardly ever hit over the fence for a home run.

In 1908, Detroit's Sam Crawford led the American League in home runs with only seven. In 1909, Ty Cobb led with nine. And most of those didn't go over the fence. They were inside-the-park homers, where the ball got past the outfielders, and the batter made it around the bases before they could throw it back in.

With such a dead ball, batters didn't swing with all their might, trying to hit home runs. Instead, they practiced bunting and place hitting. They became expert at punching line drives over the short-stop's head and slapping hard ground balls between the first and second basemen.

Wee Willie Keeler, who was five feet four and a half inches tall and weighed 140 pounds soaking wet, put it in a nutshell when he said, "I try to hit 'em where they ain't."

Under the circumstances, strategy was more important than power in baseball's early years. Teams tried to get one run at a time by bunting, place hitting, base stealing, and outthinking the opposition. Brains were as important as brawn, maybe more so.

This type of game captured the imagination of the country and grew tremendously popular. The same ballplayers who couldn't get into a decent hotel in 1900 were hailed as celebrities a decade later. By the time the United States entered World War I, in 1917, baseball had become recognized throughout the land as America's national pastime. No other sport or form of entertainment was even close.

And then, in 1920, the game changed dramatically. It suddenly switched from strategy to power, from brains to brawn. The change was due to one man and one man only. His name was Babe Ruth.

Babe Ruth and the Lively Ball

*B*ABE RUTH CHANGED THE GAME OF BASEBALL dramatically and permanently. Even with the dead ball, the young Babe Ruth hit skyscraper-high home runs that amazed his teammates and opponents as much as the fans. No one had ever hit the ball so high and so far before. Fans packed the ballparks, hoping to see him hit one over the fence.

Impressed by his popularity, the team owners decided to cash in on it. If the fans wanted to see home runs, then that's what they'd get. So, without any publicity, in 1920, the owners quietly got rid of the dead ball and substituted a new lively one in its place. It looked just like the dead ball, but when it was hit solidly it traveled a lot farther.

Baseball has never been the same since.

Within a decade, home runs started to become routine. Formerly as rare as diamonds, they became commonplace. At the same time, the arts of bunting and place hitting went into a fifty-year decline. The strategy and tactics of playing for one run at a time gave way to swinging for the fences, as teams tried to get runs quickly and in bunches.

Today, Babe Ruth is remembered primarily as a home-run hitter. That he was, indeed, but he was much more as well. For example, over his twenty-two-year career, he compiled a .342 lifetime batting average, *seventh highest* in twentieth-century baseball history. While it is true that Hank Aaron eventually did hit forty-one more lifetime home runs than Babe Ruth—755 for Aaron to 714 for Ruth—Aaron needed approximately *four thousand* more times at bat to do it.

The main reason Ruth came to bat so many times fewer than

Babe Ruth in 1927

Aaron was because for the first five years Ruth was in the big leagues—from 1914 through 1918 with the Boston Red Sox—he was a pitcher, playing only every fourth or fifth day.

He was, in fact, the *best* left-handed pitcher in baseball at the time. As a pitcher, he won twenty-three games in 1916 and twenty-four in 1917. In 1918, when the Red Sox began to put him in the outfield so he could play more often, he won thirteen games as a pitcher and simultaneously tied for the major league lead in home runs!

George Herman Ruth was born in 1895 in the slums of Baltimore, Maryland. At the age of seven, because of chronic truancy and disciplinary problems, he was sent to a Baltimore home for hard-to-control boys, St. Mary's Industrial School for Boys. It was run by the Catholic Xaverian Brothers.

He was in and out of St. Mary's for twelve years, until, at the age of nineteen, he finally left for good to play professional baseball. In later years, he always said that St. Mary's had been his real home and spoke of it with great respect and fondness.

He came to the Boston Red Sox in 1914 as a left-handed pitcher. It was as a left-handed hitter, though, that he began to attract special attention. He hit so well that by 1919 the Red Sox decided to take their best pitcher and convert him into a full-time outfielder in order to get his bat in the lineup every day.

Harry Hooper was a star Boston outfielder when Babe Ruth first joined the Red Sox. Many years later, he talked about what Ruth was like back then.

"You probably remember him," Hooper said, "with that big belly he got later on. But that wasn't there in the early days. George was six feet two inches tall and weighed 198 pounds, all of it muscle. He had a slim waist, huge biceps, no self-discipline, and not much education—not very different from lots of other young ballplayers in those days. Except for two things: he could hit a baseball further than anyone else, and he could eat more.

"Lord," Hooper recalled, "he certainly did eat too much. He'd order half a dozen hot dogs, as many bottles of soda pop, and stuff them in one after the other. That would hold him for a couple of hours, and then he'd be at it again.'"

In January 1920, the Boston Red Sox sold Babe Ruth to the New York Yankees for $125,000, surely the most foolish deal ever made in the history of baseball. In 1919, as a full-time outfielder, Ruth had set a new single-season home run record with twenty-nine homers. In 1920, with the Yankees and the new lively ball, he zoomed to fifty-four home runs; and in 1921, to fifty-nine. These would be considered remarkable home run totals even now. In those days, they were unbelievable!

With the introduction of the new lively ball, others started to clout home runs over the fence, too. But not like the Babe. In 1920, when he led the American League with fifty-four home runs, the runner-up had only nineteen. No other *team* in the league had as many home runs as Babe Ruth had all by himself.

In addition, in 1920, Ruth batted .376 and drove in 137 runs. In 1921, he hit .378 and drove in 171 runs. He proceeded to lead the league in home runs a dozen times, in runs scored eight times, and in runs batted in six times.

In the 1920s, Babe Ruth was idolized by millions, the greatest sports figure in America. He was Superman. When he hit sixty home runs in 1927 to set his famous record, it didn't create any special excitement. After all, everybody thought, he's only breaking his own record; next year, he'll probably break it again.

It did cause some controversy, however, when his salary reached $80,000 in 1930 and exceeded that of President Herbert Hoover. That was a huge sum in those days, when ballplayers didn't make anything like the kind of money they make today. When asked how he could possibly justify making more money than the president of the United States, Ruth replied in words that have been quoted ever since. "I had a better year than he did," said the Babe.

But no one can go on forever, and by 1935 Babe Ruth had reached the end of the trail. He was forty years old, more overweight than usual, could no longer run well, and his batting eye was fading. The Yankees released him in February and urged him to retire. He refused and tried to hang on with Boston in the National League, back in the city where his career had started twenty-one years earlier. But he had little success, and in May 1935, with a batting average less than his weight, he reluctantly accepted the inevitable and called it quits.

Five days before he retired, though, he turned the clock back—it had to be by sheer willpower—and gave one last glorious display of Ruthian fireworks. On May 25, at Pittsburgh's Forbes Field, he hit three mighty home runs in one game. The third, measured at over six hundred feet on the fly, is the longest ever hit in that ballpark.

Appropriately, it turned out to be his final big league hit. He trotted around the bases for what would be the last time to a thunderous ovation—although as many fans seemed to be crying as cheering.

Babe Ruth and friends

No matter how great his fame, Babe Ruth never forgot his youth at St. Mary's Industrial School for Boys. Regardless of the demands on his time, he spent countless hours cheering up youngsters in hospitals and orphanages in New York and wherever the Yankees traveled. It was often said that he appeared to be more at ease with children than with adults—perhaps because he was just a big kid himself—and youngsters everywhere spontaneously returned his affection.

Only thirteen years after he stopped playing, George Herman Ruth died of cancer at the relatively young age of fifty-three. The sorrow that was felt throughout the country was deep and genuine. Teammates and opponents almost universally said that knowing him was one of the high points of their lives.

Jimmy Austin, a longtime third baseman in the American League, played against Ruth many times. The depth of his feelings, expressed in an interview many years later, is typical of those who played with or against the Babe.

"What a warmhearted, generous soul he was," Austin said. "He was always friendly, always had time for a laugh or a wisecrack. The Babe always had a twinkle in his eye, and when he hit a homer against us, he'd never trot past third without giving me a wink. The big guy wasn't perfect. Everybody knows that. But he had a heart, he really did. A heart as big as a watermelon and made out of pure gold."

Powered by Ruth's booming bat, the New York Yankees began the dynasty that brought them eleven American League pennants and eight World Championships during the 1920s and 1930s. Ruth dominated the game and everyone in it, including many outstanding players who would have attained much greater fame were they not playing under his long shadow—for example, men such as Grover Cleveland Alexander, Rogers Hornsby, and Lou Gehrig, to name only three.

Grover Cleveland Alexander ranks with Walter Johnson and Christy Mathewson among the greatest pitchers of all time. A lanky, freckle-faced farm boy from Nebraska, he won 373 games during his twenty-year career with the Philadelphia Phillies, Chicago Cubs, and St. Louis Cardinals. That ties him with Mathewson for second place in lifetime wins in the twentieth century, topped only by Walter Johnson's 416.

A right-handed pitcher with a sneaky fastball, a deceptive curve,

Grover Cleveland Alexander

and amazing control, Alexander won thirty or more games three years in a row, from 1915 through 1917. In six other years, he won more than twenty games. In 1916, sixteen of his victories were shutouts, which is still a record.

Alexander's courage was extraordinary. He had epilepsy and achieved his remarkable record despite the ever-present threat of a seizure. At that time, there was no medication available to prevent such attacks.

Hans Lobert was the Philadelphia Phillies' third baseman for a number of years when Alex was their star pitcher. "His big problem," recalled Lobert, "was that he had epileptic fits maybe two or three times a season. He'd froth at the mouth and shiver all over and thrash around and lose consciousness. We'd hold him down and open his mouth and grab his tongue to keep him from choking himself. After a while, he'd be all right. During the years I was there, it only happened on the bench, never out on the pitching mound."

Alexander also suffered from alcoholism, which eventually destroyed him. He died in 1950 at the age of sixty-three. Two years later, Hollywood made *The Winning Team,* a movie about his life. The role of Grover Cleveland Alexander, who had been named after our twenty-second president, was played by our fortieth, Ronald Reagan.

Rogers Hornsby ranks right below Ty Cobb as baseball's all-time greatest hitter. His *lifetime* batting average of .358, over a twenty-three-year career, is second only to Cobb's .367. Since Hornsby batted right-handed and Cobb left-handed, he has the honor of being the best right-handed hitter in the game's history.

Rogers Hornsby was born in 1896 in Winters, Texas, and he had the cold gray eyes of an old-time Texas gunfighter. Those eyes became something of an obsession. He refused to read books or go to the movies for fear it would harm his eyes and affect his hitting.

Hornsby, a second baseman, led the National League in batting seven times, including a phenomenal five-year period from 1921

Rogers Hornsby in 1920, when he hit "only" .370

through 1925 when he hit (believe it or not) .397, .401, .384, .424, and .403. For the five years taken together, this averages out at .402. Even Ty Cobb never had five consecutive years quite that good! Aside from Hornsby and Cobb, no one else has ever hit over .400 three times.

But it was Rogers Hornsby's misfortune to have his career coincide with Babe Ruth's. Since Hornsby was not primarily a home run slugger—although he did lead the league in homers twice—all the publicity went to Ruth. Also, Hornsby was not a very colorful player, whereas the Babe was larger than life in everything he did.

Hornsby came to the major leagues in 1915 with the St. Louis

Cardinals, with whom he played until 1926. Thereafter, he was traded frequently, despite his spectacular batting averages, because he was a grouchy and tactless sort of fellow who had trouble getting along with people—especially managers and owners. Later, he became a manager himself as well as a part owner, and then he had similar trouble getting along with his own players.

But it is obvious from his .358 lifetime batting average that he never had much trouble getting along with opposing pitchers. Asked once if he ever feared any pitcher, he answered, "No, I feel sorry for them." Those who knew him said he wasn't boasting. In his typical blunt fashion, he was just being honest.

Lou Gehrig was the classic case of playing in Babe Ruth's shadow. As the New York Yankees' first baseman from 1925 through 1938, there was no way he could escape the big man behind him in right field. However, this never seemed to bother Gehrig. He was a shy, modest person who was content to leave the spotlight to Ruth.

Gehrig was born in New York City in 1903. After attending Columbia University, where he waited on tables to pay his way through school, he joined the Yankees in 1925 and soon became one of baseball's outstanding hitters. He is remembered by the public mainly as the durable Iron Horse who played in 2,130 consecutive games between 1925 and 1939. (This record, which many had viewed as unbreakable, was recently surpassed by Cal Ripken, Jr.) His teammates and opponents, however, remember him more for his blistering line drives and his ability to drive in runs.

For thirteen consecutive seasons, he batted in over 100 runs, seven of those times over 150. In 1931, when he drove in 184 runs, he set an American League record. He batted in a lifetime total of 1,990 runs, more than anyone in baseball history except Hank Aaron (who had 2,297) and Babe Ruth (who had 2,213). Had illness not cut him down prematurely, he probably would have added another 308, enough to top them both.

Lou Gehrig

One indication of his effectiveness when he came to bat with men on base is the twenty-three home runs he hit *with the bases loaded,* an all-time major league record.

He hit over forty home runs five times and batted over .340 eight times. A left-handed hitter, his lifetime batting average was a notable .340, tenth highest in the twentieth century.

Gehrig usually batted fourth in the Yankee batting order, right behind Babe Ruth. A reporter once mentioned to him that no matter what Gehrig did, he seemed to get almost no publicity.

Lou laughed and said, "I'm not a headline guy, and we might as well face it. When the Babe's turn at bat is over, whether he belted a homer or struck out, the fans are still talking about it when I come up. Heck, nobody would notice if I stood on my head at home plate."

On May 1, 1939, after playing in 2,130 consecutive games stretching over fourteen years, Lou Gehrig took himself out of the Yankee lineup for the good of the team. He felt weak and uncoordinated. Doctors discovered that he was suffering from an incurable rare illness, amyotrophic lateral sclerosis, now called Lou Gehrig's disease, which destroys the central nervous system. The gentle first baseman died two years later, a couple of weeks before his thirty-eighth birthday.

A widely praised 1942 movie about Lou Gehrig's life, starring

Gary Cooper, was named *The Pride of the Yankees*. The dictionary defines "pride" in this sense as "someone to be proud of . . . the best in a group." The movie could not have been better named.

During the 1930s, a number of power hitters took dead aim at Babe Ruth's record of sixty home runs in a season, which he had set in 1927, and tried their best to topple it.

Chicago Cubs outfielder Hack Wilson was the first to come close. Hack had an unlikely build for a baseball player—he was five feet six inches tall and weighed 195 pounds—but he could hit a baseball prodigious distances. He played with eagerness and enthusiasm and was a tremendous favorite with the fans.

In 1930, Hack hit fifty-six home runs, the most anyone hit in the National League until 1998, when Mark McGwire and Sammy Sosa hit seventy and sixty-six, respectively. He fell four short of Ruth's

Hack Wilson was only five feet six inches tall, but he weighed close to two hundred pounds—and when he swung, the earth trembled. This is 1930, the year he hit fifty-six home runs and drove in 190 runs.

Jimmie Foxx: 534 career home runs and a .325 lifetime batting average over twenty years

sixty, but he did set an all-time record for runs batted in that year, with the astounding total of 190.

Two great first basemen were the next to try. In 1932, Jimmie Foxx of the Philadelphia Athletics reached fifty-eight, and Hank Greenberg of the Detroit Tigers matched that figure in 1938.

Roger Maris finally did surpass the Babe in 1961, with sixty-one homers. In 1998, when both Mark McGwire and Sammy Sosa smashed the old record, both players made sure to pay tribute to the Babe and to Maris.

As the 1930s came to an end, there were two revolutionary innovations that would ultimately affect almost every aspect of the game: night baseball and television.

The first big league night game was played on May 24, 1935, when President Franklin Delano Roosevelt pushed a button in the White House that turned on the lights in Cincinnati for a night game between the Cincinnati Reds and the Philadelphia Phillies.

Most of the owners were not very enthusiastic about the idea at first. "There is no chance of night baseball ever becoming popular," one of them said, "because high-class baseball cannot be played under artificial light." But when they saw how attendance increased when games were scheduled at night, they changed their minds.

August 26, 1939, was the occasion for the first television coverage of a major league ball game. An experimental telecast was made that day of a Cincinnati-Brooklyn game played in Brooklyn. It was reported that the game could be seen on a television set "as far away as fifty miles." Hardly anyone took it seriously because television was then considered little more than a toy.

Once television really became widespread, in the 1950s and 1960s, it had a dramatic impact on baseball, especially on players' salaries and the minor leagues. Salaries began to skyrocket because the players moved into the category of TV stars. On the other hand, the minor leagues were decimated because fans chose to watch big league games on TV instead of going out to minor league ballparks. In 1949, there were fifty-nine minor leagues, with 464 teams. By 1980, only seventeen minor leagues remained, with but 155 teams. Almost all the current minor league teams are "farm clubs" of big

Two great first basemen: Lou Gehrig, left, and Hank Greenberg

league teams and are heavily subsidized by their major league parents.

Sad to say, at the end of the 1930s, one thing remained unchanged: By unwritten agreement of the team owners, black ballplayers were still not permitted to play in the major or minor leagues. This discrimination had nothing to do with ability. Black ballplayers were not even allowed to try out and show what they could do. They were never given a chance.

It is ironic, because in 1917 and 1918 the United States sent troops to Europe to fight in World War I. President Woodrow Wilson proclaimed it "a war to make the world safe for democracy." But here at home there was no democracy in America's own national pastime.

As a result, Negro leagues sprang up in the 1920s and 1930s, consisting entirely of black players. They included Satchel Paige, the legendary pitcher who many said could be a superstar in the big leagues. And Josh Gibson, who was called the black Babe Ruth because of his tremendous home runs.

But it didn't matter how good they were. Because of prejudice, the only way they could get into a big league ballpark was by buying a ticket at the box office.

Jackie Robinson Breaks the Color Barrier

DATE: April 15, 1947
OCCASION: Opening Day
PLACE: Ebbets Field, Brooklyn

*F*OR MILLIONS OF AMERICANS, BASEBALL'S MOST thrilling moment occurred at two o'clock that Tuesday afternoon when nine Brooklyn Dodgers sprang out of their dugout to take the field and start the 1947 baseball season. It was a memorable event in baseball history, indeed in American history. For the man who trotted to his position at first base was a broad-shouldered twenty-eight-year-old named Jack Roosevelt Robinson, and he was black.

The story of how he got there began five years earlier, in 1942, when Branch Rickey became president and general manager of the Brooklyn Dodger organization. The color barrier had disturbed Rickey for a long time, but he had never been in a position to do much about it. Now he was. In 1945, as World War II came to an end, he decided he would no longer abide by the owners' unwritten agreement that barred blacks from baseball.

Having made up his mind, Rickey searched the country for the ideal candidate to blaze the trail. He needed a black ballplayer who was good enough to make it in the big leagues, of course, but he also wanted someone who was mature enough to take the pressure.

Whoever he was, the first black major leaguer would have to cope with taunts and insults, with name-calling and abuse. He would have to take it all and *not* retaliate. If he fought back, Rickey reasoned, those opposed to integration in baseball would be able to say, "I told you black players can't mix with whites."

The pioneer he chose was Jackie Robinson, born in Georgia in 1919 and raised in California. Formerly a baseball, football, basketball, and track star at the University of California at Los Angeles. Formerly an officer in the U.S. Army in World War II. And at the time an infielder for the Kansas City Monarchs in the Negro leagues.

Robinson was an unlikely choice. There were no doubts about his baseball talents, but Rickey knew that he was an aggressive and highly competitive athlete who would find it difficult to accept name-calling without fighting back. However, Rickey also knew that he was extremely intelligent and would fully appreciate what was at stake.

The question was: If provoked, could Jackie control his reactions? Would he be able to keep his cool in order to pave the way for the

Branch Rickey in his Brooklyn Dodgers office in April 1947, a week before Jackie Robinson appeared in his first big league game

ultimate goal—the acceptance of blacks generally into professional baseball?

Rickey asked Robinson to meet with him in his office in Brooklyn. There Rickey told him what he had in mind and the problems involved.

"I put him through the wringer that day," Rickey said many years later. "I told him he would have to curb his aggressiveness even though he would be a target for all sorts of vilification. I predicted in disgusting detail the name-calling he would have to take and warned him he would have to take it in silence and turn the other cheek. I gave him examples: Suppose I'm on the opposing team in a close game and the two of us collide on a play. I swing at you and call you the worst name you can think of. What do you do?"

"You don't want a ballplayer who's afraid to fight back, do you?" asked a puzzled Jackie.

"I want a ballplayer with enough guts not to fight back," Rickey answered. "If you fight back, you'll play right into their hands. That's just what they want. You've got to do this job strictly with base hits and stolen bases and by fielding ground balls. Nothing else."

The meeting lasted three intense hours. Finally, Rickey stood in front of Robinson and asked, "Well? Do you want to do it?"

"Yes," answered Robinson. "I am not afraid to try."

The provocation was all that Rickey had predicted and then some. From today's perspective, it is hard to realize the depths of racial hostility back in 1947. Today, a third of major league ballplayers are African-Americans or dark-skinned Hispanics. But not in 1947. Jackie Robinson was the first.

For that, he paid the price:

- As soon as it became known that Jackie would join the Brooklyn team, four Dodger regulars asked to be traded.
- During games, a barrage of racial insults was directed at him from fans in the grandstand and from the opposing team's

bench. On several occasions, he almost lost his temper, but in each instance he remembered his promise to Branch Rickey just in time.

• A group of St. Louis Cardinals said that they would go on strike rather than play against Brooklyn if Jackie was in the lineup.

On the other hand, there were hopeful signs, too. Dodger team-mates Pee Wee Reese and Eddie Stanky gave him daily support and encouragement. Once, an angry Stanky shouted at the opposing team's bench, "Why don't you guys pick on somebody who can fight back?"

St. Louis Cardinals manager Eddie Dyer dissociated himself from some of his own players and went out of his way to wish Jackie well the first time he saw him. So did home run slugger Hank Greenberg. Around the league, a few players on every team did the same.

And Ford Frick, the president of the National League, issued a blunt ultimatum in response to the strike-threatening St. Louis Cardinals as well as to any others who might be harboring similar thoughts.

He stated: I DO NOT CARE IF HALF THE LEAGUE STRIKES. THOSE WHO DO WILL ENCOUNTER QUICK RETRIBUTION. ALL WILL BE SUSPENDED AND I DO NOT CARE IF IT WRECKS THE NATIONAL LEAGUE FOR FIVE YEARS. THIS IS THE UNITED STATES OF AMERICA AND ONE CITIZEN HAS AS MUCH RIGHT TO PLAY AS ANOTHER.

This pronouncement had such a sobering effect that within the year the worst was over and the battle virtually won. Four other black players were signed by big league teams during the 1947 season, including Larry Doby—the first in the American League—by the Cleveland Indians.

Among others, Roy Campanella joined the Dodgers in 1948, Monte Irvin the Giants in 1949, Sam Jethroe the Braves in 1950, and Willie Mays the Giants in 1951. The New York Yankees acquired their first black player, Elston Howard, in 1955. When the Boston Red Sox at long last obtained Pumpsie Green, in 1959, it finally meant that every team in the big leagues had at least one black player.

It was quite a while, however, before the first black manager was hired —Frank Robinson, by the Cleveland Indians, in 1974. (He was also the first fired—in 1977!)

Among the black players who came to the big leagues in 1948 was none other than the legendary Satchel Paige, who had been pitching in the Negro leagues since 1926. Many who had seen him in his prime claimed he

Jackie Robinson on the Dodgers' bench early in the 1947 season

was one of the greatest pitchers who ever lived, possibly the greatest. He was long past his prime, though, and it was considered a publicity stunt when the Cleveland Indians signed him on July 7, 1948, his forty-third birthday.

It was indeed good publicity because Paige quickly became the biggest box-office attraction in baseball. But it was no stunt, because he just as quickly showed that he could still pitch. Perhaps not as well as ten or fifteen years earlier, but well enough to surprise a lot of people.

After several successful appearances in relief, he made his first start in Cleveland on August 3 and won by a score of 5–3 before 72,000 screaming fans. Ten days later, he made his second start, this time in Chicago, and shut out the White Sox on five hits before a capacity crowd of 51,000. A week later, 78,000 fans in Cleveland gave him ovation after ovation as he allowed only three hits and won by a score of 1–0.

Despite his age, Satchel Paige pitched in the major leagues until 1953. In 1952, at the age of forty-seven, he won twelve games (including two shutouts) and saved ten more in relief for a next-to-last-place team that won only 64 games all season.

It has often been said that Branch Rickey signed Jackie Robinson not for idealistic reasons but because he wanted to win pennants. If so, he knew what he was doing, because Brooklyn won six pennants in the ten years Jackie was there.

The legendary Satchel Paige

In his first season, 1947, playing under incredible tension, Jackie led the league in stolen bases and was voted Rookie of the Year. In 1949, he led the National League in hitting with a .342 batting average, led the league in stolen bases, was runner-up to the league leader in runs batted in, and was voted the league's Most Valuable Player.

But statistics alone cannot give an adequate description of what Jackie Robinson was like in a baseball game, especially a close one. Like Ty Cobb, he was dynamite on the bases, distracting opposing pitchers and infielders by taking unusually long leads, threatening to steal on almost every pitch. He successfully stole

Jackie Robinson

home nineteen times, a figure exceeded by only eight players in baseball history. Since he was distinctly pigeon-toed, anyone who ever saw him running the bases found it hard to forget the sight.

During the 1949 season, he gradually began to throw off the shackles that Branch Rickey had imposed on him at that famous three-hour meeting in Rickey's office. He started to talk back, to argue with umpires, to speak his mind. He felt he had fulfilled his promise to Rickey, and now he could start behaving just like anybody else.

At about the same time, the racial name-calling from opposing benches practically disappeared, no doubt because Jackie earned widespread respect for his abilities and, probably even more importantly, because black ballplayers were being signed by other teams. After all, it wouldn't be too smart for an opponent to yell a racial insult at Jackie with a black teammate sitting near him right in his own dugout.

The breaking of the color barrier was the most significant baseball event of the 1940s, but other things were also happening at the same time. As the stars of the Ruthian era slowly passed from the field of play, a new generation of ballplayers came on the scene to replace them. It was soon evident that the three most exciting were Bob Feller and Joe DiMaggio, who came to the big leagues in 1936, and Ted Williams, who arrived three years later.

Bob Feller possessed a fastball that rivaled Walter Johnson's. Joe DiMaggio had style, courage, and leadership qualities that many say have never been equaled. And Ted Williams brought with him a superb batting eye and a striving for absolute perfection that eventually produced a .344 lifetime batting average.

Bob Feller made the most sensational debut in baseball history. An Iowa farm boy, born on November 3, 1918, he was only seventeen years old when the Cleveland Indians put him in to pitch an exhibition game against the St. Louis Cardinals in July 1936. Bob was in Cleveland on his summer vacation following his junior year in

Joe DiMaggio, left, and Bob Feller in 1936. Joe was twenty-one years old and Bob only seventeen.

high school. He wasn't even signed to a Cleveland contract. Feller promptly struck out eight Cardinals in only three innings, and he was on his way.

A month later, now under contract, he started his first big league game and struck out fifteen batters. A few weeks later, he tied the then-existing major league record by striking out seventeen batters in a game. And all before his eighteenth birthday!

A right-handed pitcher, Feller had a sizzling fastball—it was once timed at 98.6 miles an hour—and a sharp-breaking curve. He pitched until 1956 (with four years out for military service in World War II), winning twenty or more games six times, leading the league in strikeouts seven times, and pitching three no-hit games. He also pitched twelve one-hit games.

Bob Feller set a major league record of eighteen strikeouts in a nine-inning game, a feat he accomplished in 1938 at the age of nineteen. In 1986, Roger Clemens set the present record by fanning twenty men in a nine-inning game, a feat he repeated in 1996. Twenty-year-old Kerry Wood tied the record in 1998.

Joe DiMaggio and Ted Williams were just as spectacular, each in his own way. Joltin' Joe DiMaggio's career stretched from 1936 to 1951, with three years out for military service in World War II. He batted .381 in 1939 and over .300 eleven times. Nine times he drove in over 100 runs, with a high of 167 in 1937.

In 1941, he startled the baseball world by hitting safely in fifty-six consecutive games, a record that appears likely to last forever.

In the outfield, DiMaggio was a picture of poetic grace. He never seemed to exert himself, yet he was always in the right spot to catch a dangerous line drive or a long fly ball effortlessly.

Babe Ruth and Lou Gehrig had once been the heart and soul of the New York Yankees. Now it was Joe DiMaggio. Sparked by his bat, his fielding, and, above all, his example, the Yankees won ten pennants and nine World Series in the thirteen years he patrolled center field.

A popular song of the 1940s sang his praises. Ernest Hemingway,

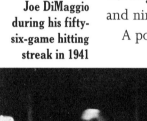

Joe DiMaggio during his fifty-six-game hitting streak in 1941

the noted author, wrote about him in his novel *The Old Man and the Sea*. Many years after he had played his last game, Simon and Garfunkel were still yearning for his return:

> Where have you gone, Joe DiMaggio?
> A nation turns its lonely eyes to you.
> What's that you say, Mrs. Robinson?
> Joltin' Joe has left and gone away.

Except for Ruth and Gehrig, no player had ever been as idolized by Yankee fans as Joe DiMaggio. In the last five years of his career, when he was an inspiration to his teammates, playing with injuries that would have put anyone else on the sidelines, thunderous applause accompanied just about every move he made on the field.

A few years after his playing days were over, Joe DiMaggio was married for a time to movie star Marilyn Monroe. Marilyn was not a baseball fan, and while she certainly knew that Joe had been a famous ballplayer, it is doubtful if she ever realized *how* famous.

On one occasion, Marilyn made a special stage appearance before nearly a hundred thousand American soldiers and received a wildly cheering ovation.

"Oh, Joe," she said later that night, "it was wonderful. You've never heard such cheering!"

Joe looked at her for a moment. Very softly, he said, "Yes I have, Marilyn."

Ted Williams of the Boston Red Sox was something else again. While Joe DiMaggio did everything instinctively, as though he had been born in a baseball uniform, Ted Williams studied and practiced morning, noon, and night. More than anything, he studied and practiced hitting, and his hard work paid off. He compiled a .344 lifetime batting average, sixth highest in the twentieth century and *the* highest of anyone who has played since the 1930s.

Williams led the American League in batting six times (including a .406 batting average in 1941 and .388 in 1957), in runs batted in four times, and in home runs four times. He hit 521 home runs during the years he played, from 1939 to 1960, even though he spent five years in the military service.

How opposing pitchers felt about seeing him come to bat is obvious. Aside from Babe Ruth, he was walked more than anyone in history—2,019 times. The Babe, by the way, received 2,056 bases on balls, only thirty-seven more than Ted.

No one has succeeded in reaching the magic .400 batting mark since Ted Williams hit .406 in 1941. Going into the last day of the 1941 season, with a final-day doubleheader scheduled, his batting average was .39955. That rounds off to .400. Boston Manager Joe Cronin suggested that Ted stay out of the lineup on the closing day of the season to protect his .400 average.

"I don't want to hit .400 that way," Ted said. "If I can't really do it, I don't want it."

In the first game of the doubleheader he got four hits, and then two more in the second game, raising his batting average to .406.

From the start, Ted Williams was a nonconformist. He refused, for example, to wear a necktie under any circumstances. When it was announced that Joe McCarthy would become the new manager of the Boston Red Sox in 1948, the players eagerly looked forward to a confrontation between McCarthy and Williams. McCarthy was known to insist that his players always wear jackets and ties in public.

On his first morning on the job, however, Manager McCarthy showed up wearing a brightly colored sports shirt. "Any manager who can't get along with a .400 hitter," he said, "has to be out of his mind."

While Bob Feller, Joe DiMaggio, and Ted Williams were making headlines in the American League during the 1940s and 1950s, the National League was growing its own superstars.

There was Stan Musial of the St. Louis Cardinals, for instance. He

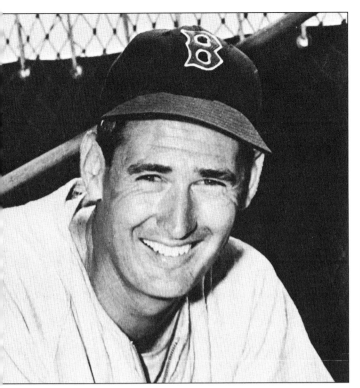

Ted Williams

**Stan Musial: a
.331 lifetime
batting average
over twenty-two
years**

batted over .300 seventeen times and finished with a .331 lifetime batting average. Musial led the league in batting seven times, and his 3,630 lifetime hits were the National League record until it was broken by Pete Rose.

And Warren Spahn, the great left-handed pitcher. Spahn won a total of 363 games, more than any left-hander in history. The only pitchers who have won more games in the twentieth century are Walter Johnson, Christy Mathewson, and Grover Cleveland Alexander. Spahn won twenty or more games thirteen times for the Boston and then the Milwaukee Braves, including two no-hitters.

In addition, four newcomers arrived in the National League in the 1950s who obviously had bright futures. Their names were Sandy Koufax, Willie Mays, Hank Aaron, and Roberto Clemente. A Jew, two blacks, and a Puerto Rican. Times certainly had changed.

"Isn't It Great Just to Be Here!"

*H*ERE'S A RIDDLE: HOW COME PITCHER SANDY KOUFAX joined the Brooklyn Dodgers in 1955, was never traded, yet played most of his career in Los Angeles?

The answer, of course, is that in 1958 the Brooklyn Dodgers moved from the East Coast to the West Coast and became the Los Angeles Dodgers.

For half a century, from 1903 through 1952, the geographic distribution of major league teams remained unaltered. During all of those years, the major leagues consisted of sixteen teams, organized as follows:

National League	American League
Boston Braves	Boston Red Sox
Chicago Cubs	Chicago White Sox
New York Giants	New York Yankees
Philadelphia Phillies	Philadelphia Athletics
St. Louis Cardinals	St. Louis Browns
Brooklyn Dodgers	Cleveland Indians
Cincinnati Reds	Detroit Tigers
Pittsburgh Pirates	Washington Senators

The first change in fifty years occurred in 1953, when the Boston Braves moved to become the Milwaukee Braves. That started a game of musical chairs.

In 1954, the St. Louis Browns turned into the Baltimore Orioles. In 1955, the Philadelphia Athletics jumped to Kansas City. In 1958,

Shibe Park, formerly the home of the Philadelphia Athletics, in 1974

the Giants moved from New York to San Francisco and the Dodgers from Brooklyn to Los Angeles. In 1966, the Braves moved again, this time to Atlanta. In 1968, so did the Athletics, this time to Oakland.

Thus, the moving vans worked overtime, generally carrying big league baseball away from the Northeast and into the western and southern states.

In the 1960s, both leagues expanded from eight to twelve teams. The National League added the Houston Astros and New York Mets in 1962 and the Montreal Expos and San Diego Padres in 1969. The American League added the Los Angeles (now the Anaheim) Angels and Minnesota Twins in 1961 and the Seattle Pilots (later the Mariners) and Kansas City Royals in 1969.

Today, instead of sixteen teams there are thirty. Only Chicago and New York remain two-team cities.

The transfer of teams from one city to another was motivated by money. Owners of teams losing money moved to where they thought they could make money. Owners of teams making money moved to where they thought they could make even more. Sometimes they thought wrong, so they moved again.

Long-distance airplane travel made it all possible. Until the early 1950s, all the major league cities were concentrated on the East Coast or in the nearby Midwest, within overnight railroad distance of one another. St. Louis was the farthest west, less than a third of the way across the country from the East Coast.

Teams traveled by train, and trains are too slow to cross the entire country in a few hours. When regular, reliable, safe, and swift cross-continental airplane service began, in the late 1940s, it was only a matter of time before teams would become more widely scattered geographically.

Not all the players were happy about the shift from trains to planes. Planes were a relatively new form of travel then, and trips were often bumpy and nerve-racking. Even today, many players are nervous when they have to fly, which is often as much as three times a week.

Boston Red Sox outfielder Jackie Jensen decided to retire early because of his fear of flying. Dodger pitcher Don Newcombe tried self-hypnosis to overcome similar fears, with only limited success.

Dodger shortstop Pee Wee Reese once tried to calm pitcher Kirby Higbe. "When your number's up, you'll go," Reese said. "It doesn't matter if you're up here or on the ground."

But that didn't satisfy Higbe. "Suppose I'm up here with some pilot," Higbe moaned, "and my number isn't up, but his is!"

Some owners of teams that were losing money made a valiant attempt to stay put by attracting more fans at the box office. Bill Veeck, the owner of the St. Louis Browns, for example, got nation-wide headlines when he went so far as to sign a twenty-six-year-old midget as a pinch hitter. Veeck figured he was a cinch to get a base on balls, and if he was put in to pinch-hit when the bases were loaded, that could force in the winning run.

Eddie Gaedel at bat on August 19, 1951. Bob Swift is the catcher and Ed Hurley the umpire.

The midget's name was Eddie Gaedel, and he was three feet seven inches tall and weighed sixty-five pounds. The number on the back of his uniform was ⅛.

St. Louis manager Zack Taylor put him in to pinch-hit in a game against the Detroit Tigers on August 19, 1951. As expected, Gaedel walked on four straight pitches, all of which were high. The next day, however, the American League banned further use of Gaedel on the grounds that it was a publicity stunt detrimental to baseball.

With the departure of the Dodgers and Giants to the West Coast in 1958, New York area fans lost two of the greatest stars of all time: Sandy Koufax and Willie Mays.

Sandy Koufax grew up in Brooklyn and joined the Dodgers in 1955 at the age of nineteen. A left-handed pitcher, for many years he had blinding speed and a good curve but no control. When he finally put it all together, in 1962, he became the best pitcher of his generation.

Koufax won twenty-five games for the Los Angeles Dodgers in

Sandy Koufax

1963, twenty-six in 1965, and twenty-seven in 1966. Twice he struck out eighteen batters in a game, tying the record Feller had set in 1938. He pitched a then-record four no-hit games and was voted the best pitcher in both leagues in 1963, 1965, and 1966.

But it ended as quickly as it had begun. In November 1966, after his best season ever and not yet thirty-one years old, Sandy Koufax announced that he would never pitch again.

A severe case of arthritis had developed in his left elbow. Before pitching, he had to be given injections, during a game his arm would swell up, and afterward his elbow had to be packed in ice. Doctors warned that if he continued pitching, he would risk serious permanent injury. So at the peak of his career, Sandy was forced to retire.

Willie Mays, on the other hand, seemed to go on forever. He came to the New York Giants in 1951 at the age of twenty and didn't stop playing until 1973. In between, he hit 660 home runs, more than

Willie Mays

anyone except Hank Aaron and Babe Ruth, stole over three hundred bases, and batted over .300 ten times.

In center field, he made acrobatic catches and threw runners out as though he had a rifle for an arm. Some veteran baseball writers believe that Willie Mays's all-around accomplishments at bat, on the bases, and in the outfield were so exceptional that he deserves to be called the greatest baseball player who ever lived—even greater than Babe Ruth, Ty Cobb, Honus Wagner, or Joe DiMaggio.

When they were both playing center field in New York, arguments arose constantly over who was better: Willie Mays of the Giants or Mickey Mantle of the Yankees. Mantle had more raw speed and sheer power than Mays—he had more raw speed and sheer power than *anybody*—but injuries hampered him throughout his career.

A switch-hitter, Mantle hit 536 lifetime home runs, 373 batting left-handed and 163 batting right-handed. From either side, his home runs traveled prodigious distances. In terms of how high and how far they went, he was in a class with Babe Ruth, Jimmie Foxx, and the Negro leagues' fabled Josh Gibson.

Mantle led the American League in home runs four times, with peaks of fifty-two in 1956 and fifty-four in 1961. His fifty-four in 1961, however, failed to lead the league because that was the year Yankee teammate Roger Maris startled the country by breaking Babe Ruth's famous record of sixty home runs in a season.

Poor Roger Maris! He never received the recognition he deserved for breaking baseball's best-known record. One reason is that he did it in the then-brand-new 162-game season, while the Babe hit his sixty homers in the shorter 154-game schedule that had previously existed. After 154 games in 1961, Maris had "only" fifty-nine home runs.

In addition, many people resented *anyone* surpassing *anything* Babe Ruth did. As Maris got closer and closer to number sixty, he was booed more than he was cheered. The booing confused and upset

Roger Maris has just hit home run number sixty-one, breaking Babe Ruth's record. Unlike Mark McGwire thirty-seven years later, Maris was not warmly embraced by the fans.

him so much he could hardly sleep at night. He got so tired, cranky, and nervous that his hair even started falling out.

Nevertheless, he refused to give up. He finally hit number sixty and tied Babe Ruth's record with four games left to play. And then, in the final game of the season, his last chance, in the fourth inning, he launched a dramatic drive into the right-field seats at Yankee Stadium for home run number sixty-one. Roger Maris never hit more than thirty-three home runs in any year thereafter.

After Maris broke the Babe's single-season home run record in 1961, other records that everyone thought were indestructible also started falling like trees in a hurricane:

- In 1962, the Dodgers' Maury Wills broke Ty Cobb's 1915 record of 96 stolen bases in a season by stealing 104 bases. Only twelve years later, Lou Brock stole 118, and then Rickey Henderson stole 130 in 1982.
- In 1965, Sandy Koufax set a single-season strikeout record by

fanning 382 batters. And only eight years later, Nolan Ryan overtook him with 383.

- As the 1960s began, only two men in history had pitched as many as three no-hit games: Cy Young and Bob Feller. But then Sandy Koufax pitched four no-hitters, followed by Nolan Ryan who went him three better with seven.
- On April 8, 1974, the Atlanta Braves' Hank Aaron broke Babe Ruth's record of 714 lifetime home runs by hitting his 715th homer. Aaron retired in 1976 with a record 755 home runs. (The legend of Babe Ruth is hard to overcome. Soon after he hit number 715, two books came out about the life of Hank Aaron, but four books came out about the life of Babe Ruth!)
- In 1977, the Cardinals' Lou Brock broke Ty Cobb's record of 892 lifetime stolen bases by stealing his 893rd base. Brock retired in 1979 with 938 stolen bases. (Rickey Henderson has since smashed this record—at the end of the 1998 season, Henderson's total stood at 1,297!)

In 1947, Jackie Robinson was the first black ballplayer to be allowed in the major leagues. One often-heard defense of the pre-1947 color ban was that black ballplayers couldn't play up to big league standards, so it was best not to hire them to begin with. Hank Aaron was thirteen years of age in 1947, Lou Brock eight years old. As Jackie Robinson trotted out to his position on Opening Day that year, who could have imagined that these two African-American youngsters would someday break the records of baseball's most illustrious heroes, Babe Ruth and Ty Cobb?

Hank Aaron was born in 1934 in Mobile, Alabama. He broke into the major leagues with Milwaukee in 1954, but it was three years before he hit as many as thirty home runs in one season. Once he started, however, he didn't stop. In fourteen of the next sixteen years, he hit between thirty and forty-five homers a year.

Aaron ended the 1973 season with 713, just one short of Ruth's

(Left)
Lou Brock: 938
lifetime stolen bases

(Right)
Rickey Henderson. His 130
stolen bases in 1982 set a
new single-season record.

record. With pressure building up all winter, he nevertheless tied the record with the *very first* swing of his bat in 1974. Such total and complete concentration is almost superhuman. And four days later, before a Monday night nationwide television audience, he hit record-breaking home run number 715 over the left-field fence in Atlanta.

Although racial tensions had lessened since Jackie Robinson broke into the big leagues in 1947, they still existed. As he approached Ruth's record, Aaron received scores of racially motivated death threats.

Lou Brock grew up in Collinston, Louisiana, one of nine children in a poor rural family. One day in school, he created a disturbance in class and as punishment was sent to the school library.

"The teacher told me to look up five baseball players," he recalled years later. "They were Jackie Robinson, Joe DiMaggio, Don Newcombe, Roy Campanella, and Stan Musial. I still remember them. Then I was to stand in front of the class and give a report on what I'd read. That's how I started to get interested in baseball."

Brock made it to Southern University at Baton Rouge, Louisiana, where he was a mathematics major until a $30,000 bonus persuaded him to leave college after his junior year for a baseball career. For twelve consecutive years, from 1965 through 1976, he stole over fifty bases a season, reaching his peak with a record-shattering 118 in 1974.

Lou Brock represented a return to the old-fashioned style of baseball—bunting, base stealing, trying to outthink the opposition—that had almost disappeared between 1920 and the late 1960s. Home runs dominated the game during those years. But the geographic expansion of the major leagues in the 1960s meant the construction of many new ballparks, a number of which were built with artificial turf on the playing field instead of real grass.

The ball behaves differently on artificial turf. Ground balls skip through the infield faster because synthetic turf is smoother than

Roberto Clemente

grass. Also, the ball usually bounces higher because artificial turf is laid, like a rug, on a fairly hard surface. Running speed became more important for outfielders so they could get to a line drive and cut it off before it skipped between them and rolled all the way to the fence for a triple or an inside-the-park home run.

Swinging for distance did not disappear, but an increasing number of players also began to concentrate on skills that had been neglected since the early 1920s.

It was no accident, then, that three of the brightest stars of the 1960s and 1970s—Roberto Clemente, Rod Carew, and Pete Rose—played the way ballplayers used to play in the early days of baseball.

Roberto Clemente was born in Carolina, Puerto Rico. A proud, moody, and, as he grew older, deeply caring man, he joined the Pittsburgh Pirates in 1955 and four times thereafter led the league in batting. He specialized in line-drive doubles and triples, where his speed was crucial, although he hit home runs from time to time as well.

He hit over .300 thirteen times, over .350 three times. In right field, his throwing arm was recognized as the strongest and most accurate in baseball.

On September 30, 1972, Clemente got his three thousandth major league hit, something only ten players had accomplished before him. Tragically, it would be his last regular-season hit in the big leagues. Three months later, on New Year's Eve, a nervous Roberto Clemente—he never did like to fly—climbed into a rickety old plane along with a pilot and three others and took off from San Juan, Puerto Rico. The plane was loaded with eight tons of desperately needed food, clothing, and medical supplies that Roberto Clemente was personally delivering to Managua, Nicaragua, which had been devastated by an earthquake a week earlier.

The airplane never made it to Nicaragua. It practically never made it off the ground. One engine exploded immediately after takeoff,

Pete Rose

followed by further explosions, and it plunged into the ocean barely a mile off the Puerto Rican coast. There were no survivors.

From a poverty-stricken boyhood, Roberto Clemente rose to wealth and fame. But he never forgot his roots, and he tried to use his money and prestige to benefit others as well as himself. He died on a mission of mercy, trying to help people in need, which is the same way he had lived.

Rodney Cline Carew was born in Panama in 1945. He was named Rodney Cline—not the most common Panamanian name—after Dr. Rodney Cline, an American doctor who luckily happened to be nearby and helped deliver him when his mother unexpectedly went into labor while on her way to the hospital.

Carew joined the Minnesota Twins in 1967. Like Clemente, his National League counterpart, he specialized in line drives. He led the league in batting seven times, tying him with Rogers Hornsby and Stan Musial. Only Ty Cobb, Honus Wagner, and Tony Gwynn have won more batting titles.

Roberto Clemente, for all his doubles and triples, also hit 240 home runs. Although Carew had over three thousand big league hits, less than a hundred were home runs. He was a true throwback to the early days of baseball.

As was Pete Rose, probably the most exciting ballplayer of his time. By combining the single-minded determination of Ty Cobb with the joy and flair of Willie Mays, Pete Rose symbolized the underlying unity of baseball from the early days to the present.

Playing with the Cincinnati Reds and later the Philadelphia Phillies, he led the National League in batting three times, in doubles five times, in hits seven times. Once, in 1978, he even hit three home runs in one game.

Born in Cincinnati in 1941, Pete Rose always played every game as though he were a rookie trying to make the team. In 1978, he hit in forty-four consecutive games, the only player to have challenged seriously the record fifty-six-game hitting streak set by Joe DiMaggio in 1941.

Only four players have hit in forty or more consecutive games in the twentieth century: Ty Cobb (forty) in 1911, George Sisler (forty-one) in 1922, Pete Rose (forty-four) in 1978, and, of course, Joltin' Joe DiMaggio (fifty-six) in 1941.

In 1985, Rose got hit number 4,192, thereby passing Ty Cobb as the major leagues' all-time leader in base hits. Only two men in all of baseball history have managed to get more than 4,000 lifetime hits—Ty Cobb with 4,191, and Pete Rose, who ended with 4,256. Next come Hank Aaron (3,771) and Stan Musial (3,630).

The glory of Pete Rose emerged in the famous sixth game of the 1975 World Series between Pete's Cincinnati Reds and the Boston Red Sox, a game that many say was the most exciting World Series game ever played. Cincinnati was leading in the series three games to two, and Boston had to win to stay alive.

In the very first inning, Boston jumped ahead 3–0. But the Reds tied it up in the fifth inning and then went ahead in the top half of the eighth, 6–3. It looked like it was all over for Boston.

In the bottom half of the eighth inning, however, with two outs, Boston's Bernie Carbo pinch-hit a three-run homer, and suddenly the game was all tied up again, 6–6.

Boston then loaded the bases in the bottom of the ninth, but Cincinnati left fielder George Foster threw Boston's Denny Doyle out at home plate to prevent the winning run from scoring.

In the eleventh inning, Cincinnati second baseman Joe Morgan smashed what looked like a sure home run, but Boston right fielder Dwight Evans made a sensational catch to keep the score tied.

Finally, in the twelfth inning, Boston catcher Carlton Fisk won the game for the Red Sox, 7–6, with a dramatic home run that bounced high off the left-field foul pole.

An inning earlier, in the eleventh inning of this thriller, Pete Rose

came to home plate for what—although he didn't know it then—
would be his last time at bat in the game. As he stepped into the batter's box, he turned to Boston catcher Carlton Fisk and home-plate
umpire Satch Davidson and grinned in delight.

"Hey, I don't know who's going to win this," he said, "but isn't it
great just to be here!"

Unfortunately, in 1989 Pete was suspended from baseball for life
for betting on ball games. Thus the all-time leader in number of hits
is not enshrined in baseball's Hall of Fame, and he may never be.

Big Randy Johnson was the cornerstone of the Seattle Mariners' pitching staff—but in 1998 the Mariners traded him to the Houston Astros for minor leaguers because they were likely to lose him to free agency.

STRIFE AND TURMOIL

*O*NCE UPON A TIME, ALL YOU NEEDED TO UNDERSTAND A newspaper's sports pages was to know the rules and regulations of baseball or football or basketball—or whatever. Nowadays, though, it's hard to tell the sports pages from the financial pages. The sports pages are filled with stories about million-dollar salaries, free agency, option years, deferred payments, union negotiations, and guaranteed multiyear contracts.

Two developments have changed baseball from the relatively simple, uncomplicated sport that it used to be to the big business that it is today. One is television and the huge amounts of money it pumps every year into the baseball industry. The other is the weakening of the "reserve clause," which used to tie a player to one club for as long as he played professional baseball—or until his club's owner sold or traded him to another club.

With respect to television, the first televised big league game was the Brooklyn-Cincinnati contest played in 1939. At that time, no one had any idea that this new technological marvel would soon revolutionize the economics of the game and make big league franchises worth fortunes.

Television did this by swelling the potential audience for a big league game from the tens of thousands who could fit into the confines of a ballpark to the tens of millions who can flick a switch and change a channel. Since a million is a *thousand* thousand, TV multiplied the potential revenues available to baseball owners by at least a thousand times. For example, instead of sixty thousand potential paying customers for a game, sixty million (which is sixty thousand times a thousand) are now available, with advertisers paying via commercials and with cable TV viewers paying directly.

If that were the only difference from the old days, it would make the owners richer, but that's about all. However, in 1975 a labor-management arbitrator named Peter Seitz ruled that the "reserve clause," which had governed baseball labor-management relations for a hundred years, was no longer sacred. That ruling, along with television, altered the economics of baseball forever.

Player contracts have contained a "reserve clause" since the earliest days of the game. The clause stated that a player *permanently* belonged to whatever club signed him first. A player could play for another team only if the club that owned his contract sold it to another club. It was called a "reserve" clause because its effect was that a player's services were permanently and unconditionally reserved to the first team that signed him, unless that team traded or sold him to someone else (technically, traded or sold his contract).

This means that if a player didn't like the salary his club offered him, there was nothing he could do about it except not play at all. Some players actually did that—sat out a year because they weren't satisfied with the club's highest salary offer. Under the reserve system, a player was not permitted to bargain with another club or to switch teams at his own initiative.

When arbitrator Peter Seitz struck down the reserve clause in 1975, in effect he made all players immediate "free agents"—that is, they became free to negotiate with *any* team for their services.

The players had organized themselves into a union in the 1960s. In the seventies, armed with the Seitz ruling, the players' union demanded that the reserve clause be eliminated from all player contracts. The owners strongly objected, arguing that without some form of reserve clause, player salaries would escalate so much as to wipe out their profits.

The conflict produced labor-management warfare, with players in the role of "labor" and owners as "management." In 1981, major league players went on strike for fifty days, wiping out a third of the schedule. The strike had been anticipated by the owners, who took out 50 million dollars of strike insurance with Lloyds of London.

In 1990, the owners locked the players out of spring training and delayed the start of the season. A strike occurs when players refuse to play; a lockout is when the owners won't let them play.

Player-owner antagonism reached a peak in 1994. In that historic year, the players went on strike in August and *stayed out*. As a result, the World Series, which had been played annually since 1904—despite two world wars and a major depression—had to be canceled. No World Series—players on strike! To most Americans, wiping out the World Series is about the same as telling a youngster that Santa Claus won't be making his rounds this Christmas. Everything considered, the 1994 strike turned out to be one of the biggest public relations blunders ever.

The players' union and the owners eventually agreed on a compromise that still exists: namely, the traditional reserve system stays in effect for the first six years a player is in the major leagues; thereafter, a player can become a free agent and negotiate with other teams if he wishes.

The avalanche of television money, combined with modified free agency, has produced skyrocketing player salaries. Many players earn a million dollars a year; some make over ten million. The highest salary Babe Ruth ever made, by the way, was $80,000.

The 1994 strike turned off millions of baseball fans. Many, disgusted at the sight of millionaires striking for even *more* money, swore they would never go to another game. As a result, major league attendance plummeted.

As we enter the twenty-first century, baseball stands at a crossroads. Eighty years ago—when it was unquestionably America's national pastime—baseball had the best of all possible worlds. Since all other team sports were in their infancy—big-time professional football didn't get started until the thirties, basketball not until the

Moises Alou was traded by his father, Montreal manager Felipe Alou, because the Expos could not afford him. He helped the Florida Marlins win the 1997 World Series and then moved on to the Houston Astros.

late forties—almost all good athletes became baseball players. Now they are just as likely to choose another sport. And since movies and the automobile were also just getting started, baseball had a near monopoly over people's leisure-time spending. Now, however, the game has to compete against a variety of attractive alternatives for the public's entertainment dollar.

Faced with these challenges, the owners and players have muffed one opportunity after another. The game on the field is as good as ever, maybe better. But baseball off the field has become a tragedy of errors.

On the field, ballplayers are bigger, stronger, better conditioned, and faster than their predecessors. They are capable of making acrobatic plays in the field that Ty Cobb and Honus Wagner could only dream of. Fastballs in the ninety-five-mile-an-hour range, once objects of wonder, have become commonplace. From the batter's box, majestic blasts regularly sail far out into space.

Off the field, though, it is a far different story. The owners ousted Commissioner Fay Vincent in 1992 because they considered him too favorably inclined toward the players' point of view. The commissioner's office remained officially vacant until 1998, when the owner who had been handling the duties—Bud Selig of the Milwaukee Brewers—took the job. Because the owners feared that any commis-

Pedro Martinez is another superlative talent developed by the Expos only to be lost to a wealthy large-market team.

Mike Piazza was traded by his beloved Dodgers, bouncing from the Marlins to the Mets to free agency. He ended up signing a seven-year, $91 million deal with the Mets.

sioner might interfere with labor-management negotiations, they left the game without leadership.

Union-owner relations remain characterized by suspicion, distrust, and hostility. Players are so enraptured by their newfound free agency that they bounce from team to team like Ping-Pong balls. Teams have thereby lost any semblance of identity—their personnel changes too much from year to year. And when players don't leave of their own accord, greedy owners get rid of them so they don't have to pay their huge salaries. The Florida Marlins won the 1997 World Series, and within weeks of their triumph owner Wayne Huizenga began scattering the players to the four winds.

An underlying unresolved issue that is not being addressed, in part because of lack of leadership, is the substantial discrepancy between the financial resources available to wealthy large-market teams (in New York and Los Angeles, for example) and relatively "poor" small-market teams (like Montreal and Milwaukee). Lots of money enables large-market teams to bid for top players, while shortages of money mean that poor teams cannot afford these players. Competition on the field will continue to be distorted until baseball adopts some form of revenue sharing that levels the competitive playing field by taking some money from the wealthy franchises and distributing it among the poorer ones. Prospects for that do not seem likely in the near future.

Whether baseball is still America's national pastime is open to debate. Basketball and football can both stake a claim. Perhaps the national pastime changes with the seasons. In any event, just when it seemed that baseball was about to totally self-destruct, new faces magically appeared on the horizon to save it.

BASEBALL MAKES A COMEBACK

*B*ASEBALL HIT THE BOTTOM OF THE BARREL IN 1994, when the players' strike forced cancellation of the World Series—the first autumn without a Fall Classic since 1904. But it is a testament to the deep-seated and lasting appeal of the game that, despite all its problems, baseball rapidly made a comeback. By 1998, only four years after the strike, the game became at least as popular as it had ever been in its long and exciting history.

A number of factors contributed to the revival of major league baseball. The most important factor, by far, was 1998's electrifying home run race: First baseman Mark McGwire of the Cardinals, right fielder Sammy Sosa of the Cubs, and center fielder Ken Griffey, Jr., of the Mariners became the focus of attention from the entire nation as they single-mindedly pursued the hallowed home run records that had been established by Babe Ruth in 1927 (sixty) and then by Roger Maris in 1961 (sixty-one). The single-season home run record is probably the best-known record in all of professional sports.

Fans packed the ballparks, hoping to see them blast the ball over the fence. Mark McGwire attracted special attention. Fans arrived well *before* game time wherever McGwire appeared, just to watch him take batting practice, hoping to see him hit a few into the bleachers even before the game started. People with little more than a marginal interest in baseball got caught up in the excitement of the chase.

For pitchers in this day and age, the most threatening figure to stride toward the batter's box with a piece of lumber in his massive fists is six-foot-five, 250-pound, redheaded Mark McGwire. Right-handed at the plate and in the field, the amiable freckle-faced first baseman is the leading power-hitter of his generation.

Mark McGwire, today's Babe Ruth

Born and raised in a middle-class environment in southern California, son of a dentist, McGwire came to the big leagues with Oakland in 1987 and was traded to St. Louis in 1997. He hit an astonishing forty-nine home runs in his rookie season, forty-two in 1992, fifty-two in 1996, and fifty-eight in 1997. Thirty-four percent of his hits go over the fence.

Over the span of twelve seasons, McGwire has hit a home run on average every 11.2 times he has come to bat. *That's better than Babe Ruth,* who homered on average once every 11.8 times at bat. The only other slugger to come anywhere close to these figures is Ralph Kiner, who on average hit a home run every 14.1 times at bat.

Saying the same thing in another way, McGwire homered 8.9 percent of the time, Ruth 8.5 percent of the time, and Kiner 7 percent.

Sammy Sosa comes from an entirely different background. A desperately poor boy in San Pedro de Macoris, in the Dominican Republic, he was struggling to earn a living for his widowed mother and five brothers and sisters by shining shoes and washing cars when he signed his first professional baseball contract at the age of sixteen.

Right-handed at bat and in the outfield, he is tremendously popular in Chicago and in all of Latin America. At six feet and two hundred pounds, he is also the smallest of the three challengers for the home run record. A regular with the Cubs starting in 1993, Sosa is no newcomer to home runs: he averaged thirty-six a season over the three-year span from 1995 to 1997.

Ken Griffey, Jr., is the glamour boy of the nineties. His talents at bat and in the outfield put him in the same class as the greatest players in the history of the game; in addition, he has a smile that says "I love what I'm doing" to everyone who watches him chase a fly ball, throw out a base runner trying to stretch a single into a double, or swing a bat with considerable authority.

Ever since ballplayers became multimillionaires, many of them

Sammy Sosa walloped sixty-six home runs and drove in a league-leading 158 runs in 1998.

Ken Griffey, Jr.,
plays with joy.

have distanced themselves from the fans. They go about their business with poker faces, showing little or no emotion, and act as though fans are a pain in the neck. They charge for their autographs—as though they weren't rich enough already—and seem to have little or no loyalty. Once they become free agents (after six years in the major leagues), they bounce from team to team like Mexican jumping beans.

Ken Griffey, Jr., is different. He plays with joy. He's the one who is responsible for the fashionable trend of wearing baseball caps backward, which is how he appears on the field in pregame batting and fielding practice. Then-Yankee manager Buck Showalter called it "bush league" but decided it was wiser to keep further such thoughts to himself after Griffey repeatedly beat the Yankees with late-inning home runs.

Junior grew up in baseball. He was underfoot in big-league locker rooms from the time he was a toddler because his dad, a highly respected outfielder with the Cincinnati Reds and New York Yankees, often brought him along when he went to work.

From a distance, Griffey doesn't look as big as he really is—six-foot-three and 205 pounds—so it is often somewhat of a surprise when his hits travel so high and so far. He hit forty-five home runs in 1993, forty-nine in 1996, and an extraordinary fifty-six in 1997, the year he was named the American League's Most Valuable Player.

• • •

It was Mark McGwire who reached the goal first. On September 7, in his team's 144th game of the season, before a capacity crowd at Busch Stadium in St. Louis and a national television audience, he drove a ball into the left-field stands to tie Maris's record of sixty-one. The very next evening, September 8, at 8:18 P.M. Central Daylight Time, in the same place, before a wildly enthusiastic roaring crowd, he launched record-breaking number sixty-two. On that date Sammy Sosa had fifty-eight homers and Junior "only" fifty.

At the end of the 1998 season, Mark McGwire had sent seventy baseballs flying into outer space, Sammy Sosa sixty-six, and Ken Griffey, Jr., fifty-six.

Although McGwire, Sosa, and Griffey were the most important play-ers behind the revival of baseball, they were not alone. Many other new stars also captured the imagination of fans across the country, including outfielder Bernie Williams and shortstop Derek Jeter, who helped power the New York Yankees to two World Series victories. In fact, the entire Yankee team—World Series winners in 1996 and 1998—contributed to baseball's revival. In 1998, they won a remarkable 114 regular season games and 11 postseason ones, and their likable demeanor made Yankee fans even out of many who had formerly been Yankee haters.

Wonderfully talented shortstops Alex Rodriguez and Nomar Garciaparra also helped bring fans back, as did sluggers Mo Vaughn, Greg Vaughn (no relation to Mo), and Juan Gonzalez. Pitcher Randy Johnson reminded fans of the best left-handed hurlers of the past, and Mike Piazza, Barry Bonds, and Cal Ripken, Jr., similarly played significant roles in baseball's resurgence.

As Griffey plays with joy, catcher Mike Piazza plays with fierce determination. Piazza is best known not for his defensive skills but for his prowess with the bat. In 1997 he hit .362, the highest batting average in baseball history by a catcher playing in one hundred or more games. Of his 201 hits, forty (or 20 percent) were homers.

In 1988, when Piazza decided to make his career in baseball, no one wanted him. He was finally selected by the Los Angeles Dodgers in the *sixty-second* round of the free-agent draft. Almost two thousand kids were chosen ahead of him. In fact, the only reason the Dodgers finally selected him was probably as a favor to Dodgers manager Tommy Lasorda, who is his godfather.

All of which is ironic, because Mike Piazza may very well turn out to be the best-hitting catcher of all time. He hits well over .300 every year—lifetime .334—and every year invariably wallops over thirty home runs and drives in more than ninety runs.

Barry Bonds, National League MVP in 1990, 1992, and 1993

Until Junior showed up, the man most experts considered the best all-around player in baseball was outfielder Barry Bonds, son of ex–major leaguer Bobby Bonds. Indeed, in recent years there has been an explosion in baseball of sons of former ballplayers. In addition to Griffey and Bonds, other sons of former major leaguers include Roberto and Sandy Alomar, Reuben Amaro, Jr., Moises Alou, Buddy Bell (as well as *his* son David), Damon Buford, Jose Cruz, Jr., Todd Hundley, Brian McRae, and Todd Stottlemyre. Also, utility infielder Casey Candaele is the son of Helen St. Aubin, a former women's professional baseball player in "a league of their own."

Born in 1964, Barry Bonds

was voted the Most Valuable Player in the National League three times (in 1990, 1992, and 1993) before he reached the age of thirty. In 1993, his best year, he batted .336, drove in 123 runs, and hit forty-six home runs.

Barry's father, Bobby Bonds, is one of a small number of players in baseball history—about two dozen—to hit thirty home runs *and* steal thirty bases in the same season. Such combinations of power and speed are rare. Willie Mays did it twice, but Bobby Bonds did it a record *five* times! Well, it was a record until *Barry* also did it five times.

For many baseball fans, however, one of the emotional highlights of the nineties was Cal Ripken, Jr.'s trot around Oriole Park at Camden Yards on the night he broke Lou Gehrig's consecutive game streak. Gehrig had played in 2,130 consecutive games, stretching from 1925 to 1939. The prevailing view was that this was one record that would never ever be broken.

But on September 5, 1995, Ripken tied the record—and on September 6 he played in his 2,131st consecutive game, a streak that had started back on May 30, 1982.

A packed house, including President Clinton and Vice-President Gore, watched as Ripken played in game number 2,131. The record was not technically broken until the game was official—after the completion of four and a half innings. When that happened, the nationally televised scene turned into a love fest. Ripken took a lap around the ballpark to the roaring applause of all the players on the field as well as the forty-six-thousand fans who were lucky enough to be there. His teammates hugged him. Players on the opposing team hugged him. His wife and children hugged him.

When the game resumed, after a twenty-two-minute standing ovation, Ripken promptly hit a home run. The scene must have been scripted in Hollywood! He added a postscript on September 20, 1998, when he voluntarily took himself out of the lineup. His consecutive game streak thus ended at an incredible 2,632.

Cal Ripken, Jr., played in 2,632 consecutive games, from May 30, 1982, through September 19, 1998. He was also the American League's MVP in 1983 and 1991.

IMPROBABLE PLAYS AND UNFORGETTABLE EVENTS

*T*HE STORY OF BASEBALL IS PUNCTUATED BY MANY strange and unusual happenings, some of which we have already encountered. No doubt the most bizarre was midget Eddie Gaedel, three feet seven inches tall, wearing number 1/8 on his back, stepping into the batter's box in a big league game. But Eddie Gaedel's moment in the sun was only one of many improbable, unlikely, and historic events that have occurred over the long time span since baseball became a part of our lives.

For example, take the day in 1917 when two opposing pitchers *both* pitched no-hitters in the same game! On that day neither Fred Toney of the Cincinnati Reds nor Hippo Vaughn of the Chicago Cubs allowed a single hit through nine innings.

As the Reds and Cubs took the field that chilly spring afternoon in Chicago, no one in the small crowd of 3,500 could have imagined that both hurlers would actually pitch no-hitters. One pitcher with a no-hitter is rare enough. The idea of two pitchers doing it in the same game is almost inconceivable. It had never happened before and it has never happened since.

Fred Toney and Hippo Vaughn (six feet four and 220 pounds) weren't the best pitchers in baseball at the time. Walter Johnson and Grover Cleveland Alexander were. But they were pretty good nonetheless—good enough so that Vaughn won twenty or more games five times in his career, and Toney did it twice.

However, even Johnson and Alexander couldn't have been better than Toney and Vaughn were on May 2, 1917. They allowed only four base runners, all getting on base by errors or bases on balls, and after

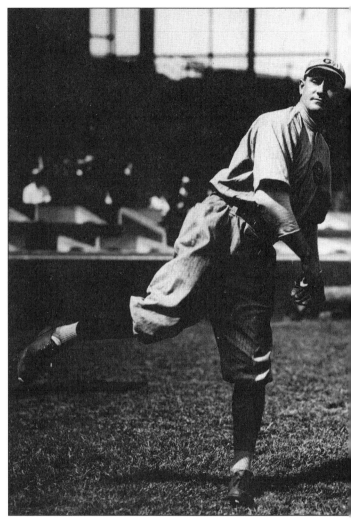

(Above) Fred
Toney and (left)
Hippo Vaughn:
two no-hitters in
the same game!

nine innings the score was tied, 0–0. In the top of the tenth, though, Cincinnati shortstop Larry Kopf singled off Hippo Vaughn for the first hit of the game, and came around to score on an error and another single. Fred Toney retired the Cubs in order in the bottom of the tenth and thus became the winner of what has to be the best-pitched game in the history of baseball.

There have been other unique pitching performances, too. Three of the most famous were by Carl Hubbell in 1934, Johnny Vander Meer in 1938, and Don Larsen in 1956.

In the first and second innings of the 1934 All-Star Game, Carl Hubbell, pitching for the National League, struck out in succession five of the most feared hitters baseball has ever known. A quiet, friendly left-hander, Hubbell was noted for his screwball, which dropped sharply as it approached home plate and also swerved in toward left-handed batters. He threw it so often for so many years that his left arm became permanently crooked from his elbow to his wrist.

King Carl Hubbell

Hubbell was known as the New York Giants' "Meal Ticket" in the thirties, when he won over two hundred games for them. As the National League's starting pitcher in the 1934 All-Star Game, he got off to a shaky first inning. The first two men he faced got on base. Coming up to bat in the third, fourth, and fifth positions in the American League batting order: Babe Ruth, Lou Gehrig, and Jimmie Foxx. The lifetime batting average for the three combined was .336. Lifetime home runs: 1,741.

But that's when King Carl, as he was also called, started to bear down in earnest. He fanned the Babe on four pitches. Gehrig went down swinging futilely. Foxx also fanned on four pitches.

But Hubbell wasn't finished. In the second inning, the first two American League batters were Al Simmons (lifetime batting average, .334) and Joe Cronin (.301). Zip-zap and they were gone too, strikeout victims like the others.

Hubbell left the All-Star Game after the customary three innings for starting pitchers, and as the game progressed the American Leaguers bombed his successors for an eventual 9–7 victory. But even though the National League lost the game, King Carl Hubbell will always be remembered for the extraordinary accomplishment of striking out Babe Ruth, Lou Gehrig, Jimmie Foxx, Al Simmons, and Joe Cronin, one right after the other.

In 1938, Johnny Vander Meer of the Cincinnati Reds pitched two *consecutive* no-hitters. Vandy was twenty-three years old, in only his first full year in the majors. On June 11 he had pitched a no-hit game against Boston and won, 3–0. Four days later the Reds traveled to Brooklyn to play the Dodgers; in fact, the game marked the introduction of night baseball at Brooklyn's Ebbets Field.

Double No-Hit Johnny Vander Meer with his manager, Bill McKechnie, left, and his catcher, Ernie Lombardi, right

The inauguration of baseball under the lights in Brooklyn on June 15, 1938, turned out to be a spectacular occasion, because Vander Meer hurled *another* no-hitter—his second in a row, a feat no other pitcher has ever matched. In the ninth inning, on the verge of immortality, he walked the bases loaded with one out (he walked a total of eight in the game), but with last-ditch determination got the next two batters. The Reds won, 6–0.

Johnny Vander Meer pitched in the major leagues for a dozen years. Overall, he won 119 games, which is a respectable total. Of those 119, 117 are forgotten, but two will be remembered for all time because no one else has ever succeeded in pitching two no-hitters back-to-back.

In the fifth game of the 1956 World Series, big Don Larsen of the New York Yankees pitched a *perfect* game against the Brooklyn Dodgers. Only about a dozen "perfect" games have been pitched in big league history, and Larsen's is the only one in World Series competition. In fact, except for Don Larsen no one in a World Series has even pitched a no-hitter, not to mention a perfect game.

What is the difference between pitching a no-hitter and pitching a perfect game? A no-hitter is just what the name says—the pitcher does not allow a single hit to the opposing team over the course of a game. He might walk some batters, or hit a few with pitched balls, or his teammates might make errors behind him, allowing members of the opposition to reach base or even score. But none of this would alter the fact that the pitcher has not allowed a base hit and has therefore pitched a no-hitter.

On a number of occasions pitchers have pitched a no-hitter and *lost* the game, because of runs scored due to bases on balls, errors, and so forth.

A perfect game is much rarer than a no-hitter. A pitcher has a perfect game if no opposing player reaches base in any way during the course of the entire game. Which means no hits, no walks, and also no errors. It is impossible to lose a truly perfect game, since it is impossible for the opposing team to score any runs if it never has any base runners.

The requirements for pitching a perfect game are really unfair to the pitcher, since he may not be credited with a perfect game because of an error that is no fault of his own. In 1920, for example, Walter Johnson pitched a no-hitter and did not walk anyone, but he is not credited in the record books with pitching a perfect game because an error by his rookie second baseman allowed an opposing batter to reach first base.

At six-foot-four and a solid 215 pounds, Yankee Don Larsen was twenty-seven years old when he took the mound against the Brooklyn Dodgers on October 8, 1956, in the fifth game of the World Series. Only a few days earlier the Dodgers had batted him out of the game in the second inning. This time, though, by the seventh inning just about every one of the sixty-five-thousand spectators in Yankee Stadium had become aware of Larsen's history-making performance, and excitement in the ballpark was mounting with each pitch.

In the ninth inning, the first two batters were easy outs, and then Dale Mitchell, a pinch hitter, came out of the Brooklyn dugout. "I was so weak in the knees at that point," Larsen recalled, "I thought I was going to faint. I was aware of the no-hitter and of the perfect game, too. I was so nervous with only one batter to go that I almost fell down. My legs were rubbery and my fingers didn't feel like they were on my hand. I said to myself, 'Please help me, somebody.'"

The count went to one ball and two strikes on Mitchell, and catcher Yogi Berra signaled for a fastball. "I blacked out," Larsen said later. "I don't remember making the last pitch." But he made it, the umpire called it a strike, and pandemonium instantly broke loose in Yankee Stadium.

Despite the fact that Don Larsen won only eighty-one games in his fourteen years in the majors and lost ninety-one (one year his record was three wins and twenty-one losses), his performance on

October 8, 1956, guarantees him a place forever right next to Christy Mathewson, Walter Johnson, and Grover Cleveland Alexander.

One of the most unusual fielding plays in baseball history is the unassisted triple play executed by Cleveland second baseman Bill Wambsganss in the fifth game of the 1920 World Series.

Unassisted triple plays are even rarer than perfect games. There have been about a dozen perfect games pitched in the big leagues,

Don Larsen making the last pitch of his perfect game in 1956. The scoreboard tells the whole story.

but only half that many unassisted triple plays, and like Don Larsen's perfect game, only *one* unassisted triple play has ever occurred in a World Series game. That one took place on October 10, 1920, in Cleveland, and again the victims were—you guessed it—the Brooklyn Dodgers.

Bill Wambsganss was often called "W'b'g'ss, 2B" in the box scores and "Wamby" in the headlines, because "Wambsganss" took up too much newspaper space. He was born in Cleveland and grew up in Fort Wayne, Indiana, the son of a Lutheran minister who expected him to follow in his footsteps.

But Bill was too shy to speak in public, which would be part of the job for a clergyman: "The trouble was I just couldn't talk in front of people, public speaking in front of a group of people, I mean. I simply couldn't do it. I was a pretty bashful youngster and I stuttered a bit, and I still remember one day I got up to make a recitation in class and I couldn't get a word out, not a single word."

But Wamby wasn't shy about baseball, and so instead of preaching from a church pulpit he ended up playing second base for the Cleveland Indians. Long after it happened, he recalled making his famous unassisted triple play in the fifth game of the 1920 World Series:

"We were playing at home, in Cleveland, and it was the top of the fifth inning. Pete Kilduff, the first man up for Brooklyn, singled, and so did Otto Miller, so there were runners on first and second and none out. The next batter smacked a rising line drive toward center field, a little over to my right—that is, to my second-base side. I made an instinctive running leap for the ball, and just managed to jump high enough to catch it in my glove for the first out.

"The impetus of my run and leap carried me toward second base and as I continued in that direction I saw Pete Kilduff still running toward third. He thought it was a sure hit, see, and was on his way to score. There I was with the ball in my glove, and him with his back to me, so I just kept right on going and touched second base for the second out.

Bill Wambsganss.
Above, he tags
Brooklyn's Otto
Miller—standing a
few feet on the
first-base side of
second base—for
the grand finale of
the most famous
triple play in
baseball history.
Hank O'Day, the
second-base
umpire, is starting
to call Miller out.

"As I touched the base, I looked to my left and there was Otto Miller, from first base, just standing there, with his mouth open, no more than a few feet away from me. 'Where did you get that ball?' he asked me. I said, 'Well, I've got it and you're going to be out number three,' and took a step or two over and tagged him lightly on the right arm. Then I started running in toward the dugout.

"It took place so suddenly that most of the fans—and the players, too, for that matter—didn't know what had happened. They had to stop and figure out just how many were out. So there was dead silence for a few seconds. Then, as I approached the dugout, it began to dawn on everybody what they had just seen, and the cheering started and quickly got louder and louder. By the time I got to the bench it was bedlam, people screaming, my teammates pounding me on the back.

"'How did it feel, Bill?' they all wanted to know.

"Well, it felt pretty thrilling and pretty wonderful. The rarest play in baseball, they say. It was more than half a century ago, but to me it seems like it happened only yesterday."

What is the most famous hit in big league history? Among the leading candidates for the honor has to be the "called shot" home run that Babe Ruth walloped in the 1932 World Series.

That he hit the home run is undeniable. But whether or not he actually "called his shot" is still, even now, a hotly debated question.

By way of background, there was a great deal of antagonism between the New York Yankees and the Chicago Cubs, the opposing teams in the 1932 World Series. During the first two games, both of which the Yankees won, the exchange of insults grew increasingly nasty. By the middle of the third game, much of the Cubs' anger seemed to focus on Ruth, who was thirty-seven years old by then and near the tail end of his long career.

In the top of the fifth inning of the third game, played in Chicago, Ruth walked to the plate with one out, the bases empty, and the score tied, 4–4. Many in the hostile crowd taunted him as a fat, over-thehill has-been, and the shouts directed at him from the Chicago dugout were savage and obscene. Charlie Root, the Chicago pitcher, got two quick strikes across. What happened then has been, and will forever be, a matter of controversy.

Ruth made a pointing gesture. Many who were there say he was pointing out to the center-field bleachers, showing where he was going to hit the next pitch. The Cubs insist he was holding up one finger and pointing out to Charlie Root to indicate that he still had one strike left—saying, in effect, that it only takes one to hit it.

Whatever he was doing then, there was no doubt about what he did a moment later—he walloped the next pitch for a tremendous home run over the center-field bleachers, the ball

Babe Ruth in the early 1930s

soaring high above the very spot to which he had apparently just pointed. It was the longest home run that had ever been hit in Chicago's Wrigley Field. The blow effectively quashed any remaining Chicago hopes, and the Yankees went on to sweep the Series with four straight victories.

But the nagging question has dragged on for more than half a century: Did the Babe *really* call his shot? The reason the question refuses to go away is because eyewitnesses themselves cannot agree on what happened. Ruth himself said that he did indeed point to the center-field bleachers, but many of the Cubs deny it—they say he was pointing all right, but toward the pitcher.

Fans and players who were there apparently saw what they wanted to see. Along with the many other secrets that have baffled mankind for centuries—like whatever happened to the dinosaurs and how did the ancient Egyptians ever manage to build the pyramids—we can now add one more mystery: Did the Babe really call his shot or didn't he?

part *Two*

Hank Aaron hitting record-breaking home run number 715 on April 8, 1974. The ball is a blur as it leaves the bat.

"You Just Keep Your Eye on the Ball"

*D*ID YOU EVER THINK ABOUT HOW DIFFICULT IT MUST be to hit a baseball thrown by a major league pitcher?

An average big league fastball travels at a speed of about eighty-eight miles an hour. The distance from the pitcher's mound to home plate is sixty feet six inches. But since the pitcher takes a stride when throwing it, the ball is actually released from a distance of only about fifty-five feet. At eighty-eight miles an hour, the ball reaches home plate in *four-tenths of a second*.

However, the batter can't wait until the ball reaches home plate to decide whether or not to swing at it. By then it's too late. He has to make up his mind *before* it arrives, deciding what to do when it is about fifteen feet away. This gives him only *three-tenths of a second* in which to judge the pitch, decide whether or not to swing (or duck!), and to start moving his bat to make contact.

Only three-tenths of a second! And that's for an average eighty-eight-mile-an-hour fastball. Bob Feller's fastball was timed at 98.6 miles an hour and Nolan Ryan's at 100.9 miles an hour.

No wonder only *twelve* men in the twentieth century have been able to hit safely as often as 34 percent of the time—that is, have a lifetime batting average as high as .340.

Here are the twelve, along with their lifetime batting averages:

Ty Cobb	.367	Babe Ruth	.342
Rogers Hornsby	.358	Harry Heilmann	.342
Joe Jackson	.356	Bill Terry	.341
Lefty O'Doul	.349	George Sisler	.340
Tris Speaker	.345	Lou Gehrig	.340
Ted Williams	.344	Tony Gwynn	.340

Even these hitters—the best in the twentieth century—*failed* to hit safely almost two-thirds of the time. Ty Cobb's .367 batting average means he hit safely 36.7 percent of the time, so he must have failed to do so 63.3 percent of the time.

George Sisler, Lou Gehrig, and Tony Gwynn hit .340, which means they hit safely 34 percent of the time and failed to get a hit 66 percent of the time.

A .300 hitter—the traditional standard of excellence in batting—succeeds in hitting safely only 30 percent of the time and fails in his turn at bat 70 percent of the time.

A player's batting average is the number of hits he gets divided by the number of times at bat, carried out to three decimal places. Every single, double, triple, and home run counts as just one hit. If a batter got a hit every time he came to bat, his batting average would be 1.000 (called batting a thousand). A player who has come to bat but has no hits at all is batting .000 (called batting zero).

In 1997, Juan Gonzalez got 158 hits in 533 times at bat for a batting average of .296 (two ninety-six). Two more hits and he would have hit safely exactly 30 percent of the time (.300).

Also in 1997, Larry Walker got 208 hits in 568 times at bat for a batting average of .366 (three sixty-six). Two more hits and he would have hit safely 37 percent of the time (.370).

Tris Speaker had a .345 lifetime batting average from 1908 through 1928 and was considered the greatest defensive center fielder of his time.

When calculating batting averages, bases on balls do not count as times at bat, so they don't affect a player's batting average. However, if a batter gets on base because of an opposing player's fielding error, it does count as a time at bat—and since it isn't a hit, his batting average falls.

• • •

Of the twelve .340-or-better hitters just listed, ten batted left-handed and only two right-handed (Hornsby and Heilmann). That is not as surprising as it looks.

Left-handed batters have advantages over right-handed batters. The most obvious advantage is that they end their swing two steps closer to first base and are already moving toward first base as they finish swinging. These two steps are important in beating out ground balls to the infield. Right-handed batters finish swinging with their momentum carrying them toward third base, and they also have to take those two extra steps in running to first base.

Another advantage left-handed batters have is that they usually hit right-handed pitchers better than they hit left-handed pitchers, and 70 percent of major league pitchers are right-handed. On the other hand, right-handed batters usually hit lefties better than righties, but only 30 percent of big league pitchers are lefties.

Tony Gwynn's lifetime batting average of .340 places him among the top twelve of the century.

Larry Walker, the National League's batting champ in 1997 (with .366) and 1998 (with .363)

Because of this fact—*left-handed batters hit righties best, while right-handed batters hit lefties best*—when a manager puts a pinch hitter into a game, the pinch hitter will almost always be a left-handed batter if the pitcher is righty and a right-handed batter if the pitcher is lefty.

For the same reason, except it's the other side of the coin, when a relief pitcher is called into a game, he will almost always be a lefty if a left-handed batter is up next and a righty if a right-handed batter is up next.

Why is it that left-handed batters hit righties best and right-handed batters hit lefties best?

The main reason is that a typical curveball naturally curves *away* from the side it is thrown from. This is because of how it is thrown and the way it spins. A curveball thrown by a right-handed pitcher curves *away* from a right-handed batter and *toward* a left-handed batter. This helps the left-handed batter because *it is easier to judge and to hit a ball curving toward you* as compared with one curving away from you.

Similarly, a curveball thrown by a lefty curves away from a left-handed batter and *toward* a right-handed batter, giving right-handed batters an advantage.

Just to make things more complicated, some pitchers throw a screwball—like Christy Mathewson, Carl Hubbell, Teddy Higuera, and Fernando Valenzuela, to name only four famed screwball throwers.

A screwball is a *reverse curve*, so things work just the opposite. Thrown by a right-handed pitcher like Mathewson, a screwball curves *toward* a right-handed batter and is thus easier for him to hit than it is for a left-handed batter to hit. Thrown by a left-handed pitcher like Hubbell, Higuera, or Valenzuela, a screwball curves toward a left-handed batter.

Since left-handed batters hit righties best, while right-handed batters hit lefties best—except when the pitcher has a good screwball—there are advantages to being a switch-hitter. A switch-hitter bats left-handed when facing right-handed pitchers and right-handed when facing left-handed pitchers. Pete Rose and Mickey Mantle are the two most successful switch-hitters in baseball history. Mantle hit 536 home runs, 373 of them left-handed and 163 right-handed.

Juan Gonzalez, the American League's MVP in 1996

A switch-hitter, however, has to keep his wits about him. Honus Wagner was fond of telling the story of Jimmy St. Vrain, a pitcher for the Chicago Cubs in the early 1900s. Jimmy, who normally batted right-handed, was a terrible hitter. To see if he might possibly do better from the other side of the plate, he tried batting left-handed one day in a game against Honus Wagner's Pittsburgh Pirates.

On the very first pitch, St. Vrain tapped a slow ground ball to Wagner at shortstop and took off as fast as he could go, but he was turned around and on the opposite side of the plate from where he was used to batting, and instead of running to first base he took off for third!

Switch-hitting Bernie Williams's .339 led the American League in batting in 1998.

Everyone in the ballpark watched in astonishment as Jimmy raced to third base, head down, spikes flying, determined to get there ahead of the throw. And Wagner, after fielding the ball, wasn't sure what to do with it himself.

"I'm standing there with the ball in my hand," Wagner said later, "looking at this guy running from home to third, and for an instant I didn't know *where* to throw it. When I finally did throw to first base, I wasn't at all sure it was the right thing to do."

In general, batters fall into one of two categories: they are either mainly *place hitters* or mainly *power hitters*. A few are both, depending on what they want to do when they come to bat, but most are primarily one or the other.

Place hitters try to slap the ball through or over the infield, trying mostly for singles and doubles and an occasional longer hit. Power hitters aim for distance, swinging for the fences.

Here are the best power hitters of all time, the fifteen who have hit five hundred or more lifetime home runs, along with the number of home runs each has hit. Their career batting averages are in parentheses.

Hank Aaron	755 (.305)		Jimmie Foxx	534 (.325)
Babe Ruth	714 (.342)		Willie McCovey	521 (.270)
Willie Mays	660 (.302)		Ted Williams	521 (.344)
Frank Robinson	586 (.294)		Ernie Banks	512 (.274)
Harmon Killebrew	573 (.256)		Eddie Mathews	512 (.271)
Reggie Jackson	563 (.262)		Mel Ott	511 (.304)
Mike Schmidt	548 (.267)		Eddie Murray	504 (.287)
Mickey Mantle	536 (.298)			

Only Babe Ruth, Jimmie Foxx, and Ted Williams are among the leaders in home runs *and* among the cream of the crop in batting average. Since power hitters swing from the heels trying to hit the ball as far as they can, their batting average usually suffers.

Almost all the old-timers who played before 1920—before Babe Ruth and the lively ball—were strictly place hitters. However, all those who have played since then are not necessarily power hitters. A quick way to classify someone as a place hitter or a power hitter is by *the percentage of his hits that are home runs.*

Of Ty Cobb's 4,191 lifetime hits, only 118, or 3 percent, were home runs. In recent years, throwbacks to the place hitters of the old days—like Tony Gwynn and Wade Boggs—still specialize in poking the ball between the infielders and spraying line drives all over the field. Only 4 percent of Tony Gwynn's and Wade Boggs's hits are homers.

Mickey Mantle hit 536 home runs and also struck out 1,710 times. The ball is a blur as Mickey grimaces at a called third strike whizzing past him.

Paul O'Neill (left)
and Chipper
Jones both hit for
power *and*
average.

At the other extreme are free-swinging strictly power hitters like Mark McGwire, Harmon Killebrew, and Jay Buhner. *Twenty-four percent or more* of their hits are home runs. If they connect safely, chances are at least one out of four that the ball will go out of the park.

Most players are somewhere in between these two extremes, but they generally tend to be close to one end of the scale or the other. In other words, relatively few are in the middle, ready to do either as the occasion warrants, with roughly 15 percent of their hits being home runs.

Here are fifteen well-known ballplayers along with the percentage of their hits that are home runs. Those in the first column are or were extreme power hitters, those in the third column extreme place hitters. Those in the middle go or went either way, depending on the circumstances of the at-bat:

Mark McGwire	34%	Larry Walker	16%	Wade Boggs	4%
Harmon Killebrew	27%	Joe DiMaggio	16%	Pete Rose	4%
Ralph Kiner	25%	Chipper Jones	16%	Tony Gwynn	4%
Babe Ruth	25%	Paul O'Neill	14%	Ty Cobb	3%
Jay Buhner	24%	Cal Ripken, Jr.	13%	Joe Sewell	2%

A lot of mainly (but not extreme) power hitters are around the 20 percent mark—about 20 percent of their hits are home runs—including Mickey Mantle, Ken Griffey, Jr., Willie Mays, Hank Aaron, Mike Piazza, Frank Thomas, and Ted Williams.

A lot of mainly (but not extreme) place hitters are around the 10 percent level—about 10 percent of their hits are home runs—including Kirby Puckett, Rogers Hornsby, Bernie Williams, Jackie Robinson, and Roberto Clemente.

It isn't necessarily better to be a power hitter or a place hitter provided you're good at whatever you are. After all, Babe Ruth is in the first column, Joe DiMaggio is in the second, and Ty Cobb is in the third. Each is a different kind of hitter, but each has a claim to being

Joe Sewell, the hardest man to strike out in baseball history

one of the greatest of all time.

Although it isn't necessarily better to be one rather than the other, there are definite differences among them. With such notable exceptions as Babe Ruth, Ted Williams, and Jimmie Foxx, power hitters generally have lower batting averages than the others. On the other hand, extreme place hitters have higher batting averages.

However, it's the power hitters who drive in the runs. Harmon Killebrew batted in one hundred or more runs nine times and Ralph Kiner six times. Among the place hitters in the third column, Wade Boggs and Pete Rose never did have as many as one hundred runs batted in, Tony Gwynn has done it only once, and Joe Sewell twice.

Power hitters have one failing they cannot seem to control: They strike out a lot. Mark McGwire, in the first column, strikes out once out of every four times he comes to bat; Harmon Killebrew fanned once in every five times; Babe Ruth, once in every six times; and Ralph Kiner, once in every seven times he came to bat. The all-time leader in career strikeouts is Reggie Jackson, with 2,597. Babe Ruth fanned 1,330 times.

Compare that with the extreme place hitters. Tony Gwynn strikes out once in every twenty-one times he comes to bat, Ty Cobb struck out once out of every thirty-two times, and Joe Sewell once out of every sixty-three times he came up to the plate.

Indeed, Joe Sewell was the toughest man to strike out in baseball history. Shortstop for the Cleveland Indians from 1920 to 1928 and third baseman for the Indians and the New York Yankees from 1929 to 1933, he compiled a .312 lifetime batting average as he came to bat a total of 7,132 times and struck out only 114 times. In 1925, he batted 608 times and struck out on only four occasions.

Those who seek advice from the experts so they can learn the secret of success are frequently doomed to disappointment. The experts often do things so naturally, like tying one's shoelaces, that they have trouble explaining it to others. A teammate once asked Joe Sewell the secret of how he avoided striking out.

Sewell stammered, not sure what to say. "Well," he finally answered, trying to be helpful, "you just keep your eye on the ball."

Easier said than done when it's coming toward you at ninety miles an hour and you've got only three-tenths of a second to make your move!

Roger Clemens, five-time American League Cy Young Award winner (1986, 1987, 1991, 1997, and 1998)

"I Lost My Fastball"

CONNIE MACK, WHO MANAGED IN THE BIG LEAGUES for fifty years (yes, fifty years!), used to say that pitching is 75 percent of baseball. Other experts have put the figure even higher, some as high as 90 percent. While that might be going too far, it is generally agreed that good hitting by itself cannot win pennants but that good pitching can.

In 1930, for example, the Philadelphia Phillies had a *team* batting average of .315. They scored an average of six runs a game. But they allowed the opposition an average of eight runs a game and finished in last place. In 1947, the New York Giants hit a record 221 home runs and couldn't finish any higher than fourth.

On the other hand, the 1988 Los Angeles Dodgers had a team batting average of .248 and hit only ninety-nine home runs all year. But with Orel Hershiser pitching, they won both the pennant and the World Series.

It is also generally agreed that good pitchers can usually stop good hitters. Ted Williams often said that hitting a baseball properly is the single most difficult thing to do in all of sports. If so, pitching a baseball properly must be the second most difficult thing.

Only four pitchers in the twentieth century have managed to win as many as 350 games. Here are the four and their lifetime victory totals:

Walter Johnson	416
Grover Cleveland Alexander	373
Christy Mathewson	373
Warren Spahn	363

One pitcher in history *did* win more games than Walter Johnson— Cy Young, who won 511. The annual award for the best pitcher in each league is named after him. However, he won over half his games before 1900.

Some others who might have won 350 games were unfortunately prevented from doing so by things outside their control. Bob Feller, for instance, won 266 games. However, he was in the military service for almost four years during World War II, when he was at the peak of his career.

The year before he left, he won twenty-five games, and the year he returned he won twenty-six. If he had won just twenty-one games a season the four years he was gone, he would have ended his career fifth on the all-time list, right behind Warren Spahn.

And imagine how many games Sandy Koufax might have won if he hadn't been forced to retire before his thirty-first birthday because of arthritis. Even so, he still won 165 games, 111 of them in his last five years. In that five-year period, 1962 through 1966, Koufax had an *earned run average* (ERA) of 1.95, which means he allowed the opposition an average of slightly less than two earned runs a game.

The number of games a pitcher wins is affected not only by how well he pitches but also by what his teammates do—for example, how many runs they get him. For that reason, the best measure of a pitcher's ability is his ERA. This is the average number of earned runs he allows the opposition over nine innings.

For purposes of figuring a pitcher's ERA, "unearned" runs are separated from "earned" runs, although one kind of run is just as good as another when it comes to winning a ball game. An unearned run is one that is due to a fielding error, so it isn't really the pitcher's fault.

A pitcher's ERA is calculated as the number of earned runs he allows divided by the number of innings he pitches. The result is the average number of earned runs allowed in an inning. This figure is multiplied by nine in order to convert it to nine innings. Thus it gives the average number of earned runs allowed in a nine-inning game.

ERAs are carried out to two decimal places.

An easier way to do the exact same thing is simply to multiply a pitcher's earned runs by nine and divide the result by the number of innings pitched. If a pitcher allows ten earned runs in forty-five innings, for example, multiply 10 by 9 = 90 and divide by 45 = 2.00. On average, the pitcher has allowed exactly two earned runs a game.

In 1997, Roger Clemens of the Blue Jays allowed sixty earned runs in 264 innings. Multiply 60 by 9 = 540 and divide by 264 = 2.045, which rounds off to an ERA of 2.05. In other words, Clemens allowed opponents an average of slightly more than two runs a game. He won the Cy Young Award as the best pitcher in the American League that year.

Greg Maddux, four-time National League Cy Young Award winner (1992 through 1995)

Or take Greg Maddux: in 1994, when he won the Cy Young Award as the best pitcher in the National League, he allowed only 35 earned runs in 202 innings. Multiply 35 by 9 = 315 and divide by 202 = 1.56. Maddux allowed the opposition about one and a half earned runs a game that year.

An ERA under 3.00 is considered excellent, and one under 2.00 is fantastic. Roger Clemens and Greg Maddux are in the 1990s what Christy Mathewson and Walter Johnson were many years ago—the two best pitchers in the game.

Here are twenty great pitchers and the ERA of each for *the five con-secutive years during each pitcher's career when his ERA was lowest.* All four of the 350-game winners are here, plus sixteen more all-time superstars:

Walter Johnson	1.49	Carl Hubbell	2.40
Grover C. Alexander	1.64	Lefty Grove	2.56
Christy Mathewson	1.69	Roger Clemens	2.62
Sandy Koufax	1.95	Bob Feller	2.68
Greg Maddux	2.06	Orel Hershiser	2.69
Babe Ruth	2.16	Dazzy Vance	2.76
Juan Marichal	2.30	Steve Carlton	2.77
Tom Seaver	2.35	Warren Spahn	2.87
Jim Palmer	2.35	Nolan Ryan	2.94
Bob Gibson	2.35	Dizzy Dean	2.95

Warren Spahn, a lifetime 363-game winner

Some pitchers from every era are included in the twenty. Except for Sandy Koufax and Greg Maddux, the first six pitched with the dead ball—that is, before 1920—which helps account for their very low ERAs. Koufax's five-year ERA of 1.95 is the best since the lively ball was introduced in 1920. Indeed, it is one of the best five-year pitching records in the entire twentieth century, regardless of the ball being lively or dead.

Babe Ruth, by the way, seems to pop up everywhere. He is near the top of every list, whether it involves batting average, home runs, or pitching excellence.

Of the twenty great pitchers listed, fourteen are right-handers and six left-handers. The lefties are Sandy Koufax, Babe Ruth, Carl Hubbell, Lefty Grove, Steve Carlton, and Warren Spahn. This is what might be expected, since about 70 percent of major league pitchers are right-handers.

Left-handed pitchers are often called "southpaws." Do you know why? Because baseball fields are traditionally laid out so that the batter looks to the east as he faces the pitcher. This is to prevent the setting sun (which of course always sets in the west) from getting in the batter's eyes. If second base is east and home plate west, then third base has to be to the north and first base to the south. Since a left-handed pitcher throws from the first-base (or southern) side of the pitching mound, he's called a southpaw.

Who was the greatest left-handed pitcher of all time? Opinions differ on this, as they do on virtually everything else in baseball, but the three leading candidates for the honor are Lefty Grove, Warren Spahn, and Sandy Koufax.

Babe Ruth as a left-handed pitcher with the Boston Red Sox in 1916

Bob Feller

Juan Marichal

Robert Moses "Lefty" Grove starred in the twenties and thirties for the Philadelphia Athletics and the Boston Red Sox; in 1930 and 1931, combined, he won fifty-nine games and lost only nine. Warren Spahn won more games than any other lefty in baseball history—363— mostly for the Boston and Milwaukee (now the Atlanta) Braves in the fifties and sixties. And there's no telling what records Sandy Koufax would have set if he hadn't been forced to retire so early.

• • •

Just as some batters are mainly power hitters, some pitchers are mainly power pitchers. There are very few of them, however. The few who are mainly power pitchers rely primarily on their blazing speed. To get away with it, their fastball has to reach ninety-three to ninety-five miles an hour regularly and consistently, and have some "movement" on it as well. If a fastball is perfectly straight and doesn't move a little up or down as it approaches home plate, good hitters will learn to time it and tee off on it.

Included in that small elite group are Walter Johnson, Dazzy Vance, Lefty Grove, Bob Feller, Sandy Koufax, Roger Clemens, Randy John-

Curt Schilling led the National League in strikeouts in 1997 (with 319) and in 1998 (with 300).

son, and Nolan Ryan. They simply overpower batters with their speed, racking up large numbers of strikeouts in the process. (Pitchers who are not mainly power pitchers can record substantial numbers of strikeouts, too, but they do it more by deception than by raw speed, and their strikeout totals are usually considerably less.)

Walter Johnson led the league in strikeouts twelve times, Nolan Ryan ten times, and Vance, Grove, and Feller seven times each. Even mainly power pitchers, however, usually develop a curve and change of pace (or slow ball), so that the contrast makes their fastball look even faster.

Although Walter Johnson and Lefty Grove went through most of their careers without much of a curve, Dazzy Vance, Bob Feller, Sandy Koufax, and Nolan Ryan all perfected outstanding curves that eventually became as important as their fastball. The combination of a blazing fastball *and* a sharp-breaking curve, along with a change of pace, made them practically unhittable when everything was working right.

John Wetteland, one of the premier relievers of the '90s

Does a curveball *really* curve, or is it an optical illusion? This question used to be debated all the time. Now it is generally agreed that the spin a pitcher puts on a baseball by snapping his wrist when he releases the ball really does make it curve. This conclusion is supported by proof from the principles of physics and aerodynamics.

And, of course, all pitchers, no matter what kind, need *control*— the ability to throw the ball where they want to when they

When Kerry Wood struck out twenty batters in a nine-inning game on May 6, 1998, the twenty-year-old tied Roger Clemens's record.

want to. For a pitch to be in the strike zone, it must be over home plate and between the middle of the batter's chest and the top of his knees when he is in his normal batting stance.

Before Eddie Gaedel, the three-foot-seven-inch midget, came to bat in 1951, St. Louis owner Bill Veeck taught him to crouch over as much as possible when taking his batting stance. The result was a strike zone that measured exactly one and a half inches!

However, when Eddie actually came up to bat, he ignored Veeck's instructions and stood more or less straight up, with his feet spread wide, imitating Joe DiMaggio's batting stance. He walked on four straight pitches anyway.

When ballplayers sit around and talk among themselves and the subject of control comes up, sooner or later Steve Dalkowski's name is sure to be mentioned. Although most baseball fans never heard of him, Steve Dalkowski is a legend among ballplayers.

A left-handed pitcher from New Britain, Connecticut, Dalkowski is said to have been the fastest pitcher who ever lived, with no exceptions. Those who saw him swear that his fastball flashed by at *over* 110 miles an hour!

Dalkowski pitched in the minor leagues from 1957 through 1965 but never made it to the big leagues because he could not master control. In nine years in the minors, he pitched about 1,000 innings and struck out 1,400 batters. But he walked as many as he struck out, so that his lifetime ERA was 5.59. He lost almost twice as many games

Steve Dalkowski

as he won and quit baseball in disgust at the age of twenty-six.

Feller, Koufax, Randy Johnson, and Nolan Ryan all had control problems, too, at one time or another. Randy Johnson led the league in bases on balls three times, Feller four times, Ryan eight times. Ryan also led the league in wild pitches five times.

Even pitchers who do not rely primarily on their fastball, and that includes most of them, need at least an eighty-three- to eighty-five-mile-an-hour fastball to pitch successfully in the big leagues.

Without it, batters of major league quality would soon learn to anticipate their "breaking" pitches—such as their curve, slider, screwball, knuckleball, sinker, or what have you—and hit them solidly. By mixing up their pitches—sometimes a curve, occasionally a fastball, unexpectedly a slow ball or change of pace—they throw the batter's timing off, making all of their pitches more difficult to hit.

Gene Conley, who pitched for the Braves, Phillies, and Red Sox in the 1950s and early 1960s, was one of the tallest pitchers in the history of the game. He was six feet eight inches tall and weighed 225 pounds. For a number of years, he played professional basketball with the Boston Celtics when the baseball season ended and then returned to big league baseball when the basketball season finished.

Although he was not mainly a fastball pitcher, Conley realized the importance of his fastball in making all his pitches effective. In 1964, he hurt his arm and could no longer put much speed on his pitches. After months of trying, he finally gave up, and years later he described how he felt at the time.

"I walked into a church," he recalled, "and sat down in the back, all by myself. There was a service going on. All of a sudden, it hit me real hard, and I started crying. I just sat there in that last row and cried and cried, trying to keep my head down so as not to upset anybody. Then I felt a hand on my shoulder, and I looked up. An elderly gentleman was standing there, gazing down at me. 'What's the matter, son?' he asked. 'Did you lose your mother?' I shook my head, the tears still running. 'No, sir,' I said. 'I lost my fastball.'"

Nolan Ryan, the only man ever to pitch seven no-hitters

"WHAT NIGHT SHALL WE MAKE IT, AL?"

*F*IELDING IS THE MOST UNDERRATED PART OF BASEBALL. Great hitters and great pitchers become famous, but great fielders don't even make it to the big leagues unless they can also hit reasonably well.

Mike Gonzalez, a Cuban-born scout for the St. Louis Cardinals in the 1930s, spoke only broken English. Once he sent a famous telegram back to St. Louis after scouting a minor league prospect: "Good field, no hit," read the telegram, and that was the end of that prospect.

Defense is rarely as spectacular as offense no matter what the sport. But good fielding *does* win ball games just as poor fielding loses them.

The defensive brilliance of third baseman Brooks Robinson of the Baltimore Orioles was crucial in winning the 1970 World Series. The same is true of the sparkling defensive play of Yankee third baseman Graig Nettles in the 1978 World Series. On the other hand, a line drive misjudged by St. Louis Cardinals center fielder Curt Flood was the turning point in the seventh game of the 1968 World Series when the Detroit Tigers beat the Cardinals by a score of 4–1 to win the series.

Let's consider the defensive positions one by one and examine each in turn.

The *catcher* is the defensive field general of a baseball team. Although the protective equipment he wears is often called "the tools of ignorance," in fact the catcher has to be one of the smartest players on the team. That is because it is usually the catcher, rather than the pitcher, who decides what kinds of pitches to throw to each batter.

Baseball people say that the catcher "calls" the game—that is, he "calls" (via hand signals) for the pitcher to throw a fastball, or a curve, or a screwball, or whatever. If the pitcher disagrees, he lets the catcher know about it, usually by shaking his head, and then the catcher will probably call for something else. In any event, it is generally the catcher, not the pitcher, who makes the initial decisions, which is why a smart catcher is so valuable to a ball club.

Catcher Thurmon Munson tensely awaits both the ball and the base runner, who has rounded third and is racing for home.

To call a game well, a catcher has to know the strengths and weaknesses of all the opposing batters and the strengths and weaknesses of his own pitchers. He evaluates one against the other when deciding what pitch to call for under differing circumstances.

The catcher also has to be able to stop low pitches that hit the ground before they reach him. Since a lot of pitchers are low-ball pitchers—that is, their most effective pitches cross home plate around the batter's knees and are dropping when they cross the plate—the ball frequently hits the ground before it gets to the catcher. It takes considerable skill to catch or block such pitches so they don't get by and allow base runners to advance.

Josh Gibson, home run king of the Negro leagues, also possessed a rifle arm from behind the plate.

And, above all, a catcher must have a superb throwing arm in order to prevent base runners from stealing. The distance from home plate to second base is 127 feet, 3 inches. If a catcher can't make that throw on a line, like a bullet, he'll never be able to stop good base runners from stealing second whenever they feel like it.

Often catchers try to distract the batter by talking to him when he is up at bat. The New York Yankees' Yogi Berra, for example, kept up a steady stream of conversation with one batter after another.

A classic story concerns Boston catcher Al Spohrer, who once tried to distract the great Rogers Hornsby by talking about one of Hornsby's favorite subjects—food.

"Say, Rog," said Spohrer when Hornsby came to bat with two men on base in a close game, "my wife has discovered a butcher who has fantastic steaks."

"Is that so?" responded Hornsby.

"Strike one!" the umpire said.

"Not only that, Rog, but you know how great a cook my wife is," continued Spohrer.

"Strike two!" said the umpire.

"We thought," Spohrer went on, "that maybe you'd like to come over to the house and have dinner with us some night."

Crack! Hornsby walloped the ball over the left-field fence and then trotted around the bases. As he crossed home plate, he turned toward a dejected Spohrer.

"What night shall we make it, Al?" he asked.

Slugger Mo Vaughn held down first base for the Red Sox until signing with the Angels in 1998. He usually hits well over .300 every year and also drives in more than a hundred runs.

The *first baseman* is often a slugger whose fielding might leave something to be desired. Nevertheless, there have been many good-hitting *and* sharp-fielding first basemen in baseball history. A good-fielding first baseman can add a great deal to a team's defense, because many left-handed batters hit hard ground balls somewhere in the neighborhood of first base. A first baseman who can snare these and turn them into outs will prevent a lot of runs from scoring.

The main job of the first baseman, however, is to be a vacuum cleaner in gobbling up poor throws. Many of the throws to him are in the dirt or wide or high because they come from infielders who are off balance when they hurriedly release the ball. If a first baseman can't handle wild throws that are reachable, he won't last long in the big leagues. Not at first base, anyway.

The first baseman must also have the flexibility of a ballet dancer because he has to stretch as far as humanly possible when receiving throws from the other infielders who are trying to get the ball to him before the runner arrives at first base. The farther he stretches, the quicker the ball reaches his glove, and in many plays at first base only a fraction of a second is the difference between safe and out.

It is desirable, but not absolutely necessary, that a first baseman throw left-handed. It is easier, and quicker, for a left-handed first baseman to pick up a bunt or a ground ball and throw to second base to start a first-to-second-to-first double play.

If you stop to think about it, you take a forward step with your *left foot* when you throw *right-handed*. And you similarly take a forward step with your *right foot* when you throw *left-handed*.

When a left-handed first baseman picks up a ground ball, his *right* foot is already on his second-base side. So all he has to do is throw the ball to second base. But when a right-handed first baseman picks up a ground ball, his *left* foot is on the wrong side; it is on the first-base side. So he has to turn completely around to throw to second base.

Nevertheless, some of baseball's greatest first basemen were right-handed—including Jimmie Foxx, Hank Greenberg, and Mark McGwire.

The *second baseman* has to be an acrobat with nerves of steel. He has to be able to execute a double play even though he knows a base runner he can't see may crash into him momentarily. He has to be a sure fielder on ground balls, of course, and able to range far to either his right or left. But what distinguishes the best second basemen from the merely good ones is their ability to make the "routine" short-to-second-to-first double play.

On this most common of all double plays, the shortstop fields a ground ball and tosses it to the second baseman, who steps on second and relays the ball to first. As the second baseman takes the toss from the shortstop, his back or left side is toward first base, so he cannot see how close the base runner from first base is to him. But he knows that something resembling a freight train is approaching and may smash into him at any second. Despite this, he has to touch second base, jump over the sliding base runner, and throw to first base all at once.

Unlike the first baseman, the second baseman has no choice: He *must* throw right-handed. Otherwise, he could never make that particular play quickly enough. Since his left foot is already closer to first base than his right foot when he touches second base, a right-handed second baseman doesn't have to turn all the way around before relaying the ball to the first baseman.

A lot of times, the second baseman doesn't actually *touch* second base on that play. But as long as he comes fairly close, the umpire usually lets him get away with it. Umpires have a certain amount of

Jerry Coleman of the Yankees shows why a second baseman has to be an acrobat with nerves of steel. (The base runner, out at second as the first part of a double play, is Jerry Scala of the White Sox.)

sympathy for the second baseman and give him a break—they know that if the second baseman doesn't get out of the way quickly, he'll be flattened by the oncoming base runner, who is eager to break up the double play. These are called "phantom" double plays, but they count just as much as the "real" ones.

When the *shortstop* is the middle man on a double play, at least he is facing first base and can see the base runner coming toward him. In all other respects, however, the shortstop has the toughest job in the infield. Since about two out of every three hitters bat right-handed, more ground balls are hit into the shortstop's territory than anywhere else.

In fact, the shortstop is so important defensively that he is an exception to the rule that great fielders don't make it to the big leagues unless they can also hit reasonably well. A brilliant defensive shortstop can last for years in the major leagues even if he isn't very productive on offense. (Sometimes that holds for a very good defensive catcher, too.)

The crucial play for a shortstop, the one play that separates a truly great shortstop from all the rest, is fielding a ground ball deep "in the hole," that is, far back and well over to his right. This requires speed, agility, and an exceptionally long and strong throw to first base, a throw of about 130 or 135 feet. He has to backhand the ball while running *away* from first base, set himself, and fire it to the first baseman with enough power so it gets there ahead of the runner.

Like second basemen, shortstops *must* throw right-handed. Otherwise, they could never make that particular play in time. Since their left foot is already closer to first base than their right foot on that play, right-handed shortstops don't have to waste time turning all the way around before throwing the ball to the first baseman.

The introduction of artificial turf has made all the defensive positions more difficult to play than they used to be because ground balls roll much faster on synthetic turf than they do on grass. All the infielders have to play farther back on artificial turf than on grass, or else the ball is past them before they have time to react. On the other hand, they worry less about bad hops on artificial turf.

Cincinnati shortstop Dave Concepcion devised an ingenious way of using artificial turf to his own advantage. On long throws from deep in the hole, he perfected the tactic of deliberately throwing the ball into the turf about fifteen feet in front of the first baseman, letting one long bounce carry it the rest of the way. This isn't possible on grass except as a last resort because the bounce isn't as true and the ball rarely accelerates when it hits real grass the way it often does when it hits artificial turf.

Although speed is an asset to a shortstop, knowledge about where to play the batters can compensate to a great extent when a shortstop isn't too fast afoot. Indeed, all good fielders, no matter what position they play, depend as much on their knowledge of *where* to play each batter as on anything else. They will shift several feet to the right or left or backward or forward, depending on the batter's typical hitting pattern, the pitcher's characteristics, the type of pitch coming up, and any other factors that could influence where the ball might be hit.

The 1990s is the era of super shortstops. Most shortstops have earned their salaries by their fielding skills. But shortstops Nomar

Slick-fielding shortstop Alex Rodriguez also hits for both average and power.

Garciaparra, Derek Jeter, Barry Larkin, and Alex Rodriguez are powerful hitters *as well as* slick fielders. As a group, they are the best in baseball history.

The *third baseman* has to have an instantaneous reaction time because many of the balls hit to him are line drives or very hard grounders that reach him in a flash. He either grabs the ball almost instinctively, or he doesn't.

Pepper Martin, who played third base for the St. Louis Cardinals in the 1930s, used his chest as much as his glove in fielding his position. He'd block the ball with his body, pounce on it, and throw to first base.

The third baseman's most difficult play is a bunt or slow roller down the third-base line. He has to dash in, grab the ball with his bare hand, and whip it over to first base, all in one fluid motion. Again, third basemen have to throw right-handed. Otherwise, they would have no chance of executing that play in time to get the run-

Baltimore third baseman Brooks Robinson makes what was for him a routine play.

ner. Since a third baseman's left foot is closer to first base than his right foot, a right-handed third baseman doesn't have to turn all the way around to throw the ball to first base.

There have been only a few great fielding third basemen in history because the position is often filled—like first base—with a good hitter whose fielding is only passable. Pie Traynor, of the Pittsburgh Pirates in the 1920s and early 1930s, was one of the best. At the time the saying was "Twice Hornsby doubled down the left-field line and twice Traynor threw him out."

Other outstanding fielding third basemen include Billy Cox of the Brooklyn Dodgers, Brooks Robinson of the Baltimore Orioles, Clete Boyer and Graig Nettles of the New York Yankees, and Mike Schmidt of the Philadelphia Phillies.

The *outfielders* are generally the big hitters. A good-fielding outfielder can be enormously helpful to a team, but good hitters who can't field have to be fitted in *somewhere*. Unless they're designated hitters, who never play defensively, they usually wind up in the outfield—especially if they throw left-handed and can't play first base. (Actually, *anyone* who throws left-handed and can't pitch or play first base will necessarily wind up in the outfield.)

The best outfielder—usually the fastest—will generally be the *center fielder*. He has the most territory to cover, and if the right and left fielders are not fully reliable, the center fielder will have to patrol a good deal of right-center and left-center as well as center field itself. He has to be fast, able to come in for balls hit over the second baseman's and shortstop's heads, able to go back for long fly balls, and have a good enough arm to make long and accurate throws to third base and home plate when needed.

Many believe that Willie Mays was the greatest defensive center fielder of all time. His most famous catch was in the 1954 World Series when Cleveland's Vic Wertz hit a towering fly ball 445 feet to deep center field. Running at top speed with his back to home plate, Mays

Willie Mays snares Vic Wertz's 445-foot drive to deep center field in the 1954 World Series.

caught it over his left shoulder and in one fluid motion whirled around and threw the ball back to the infield. Instead of two men scoring, none did, and the Giants went on to win the game and the Series.

Actually, the *right fielder* needs to have an even *better* arm than the center fielder, since he frequently has to make the very long throw from right field to third base to keep base runners from going from first to third on a single. Babe Ruth, Roberto Clemente, Carl Furillo, and Al Kaline all played right field most of the time because of their exceptional throwing abilities.

By the way, it isn't just the distance that is important on a long throw from the outfield. Equally important is the trajectory—that is, the throw shouldn't be a high one that arcs like a rainbow from the outfielder to its destination. It should be a *low* throw, on a line about seven or eight feet high almost its entire length so that an infielder (the cutoff man) can interrupt it and redirect it somewhere else if necessary. Long, high throws that miss the cutoff man often impress the crowd, but the manager will be less enthusiastic.

The *left fielder* will often be the team's weakest fielder both in terms of speed and throwing proficiency. This doesn't mean that all left fielders are poor defensive outfielders. Far from it. But if a team does happen to have a hard-hitting outfielder who isn't too fast and can't throw too well, he'll be its designated hitter or left fielder.

Artificial turf puts even more pressure on outfielders than on infielders. Since the ball moves so much faster on artificial turf than on grass, outfielders have to be faster than ever to stop it from getting past them. What would ordinarily be a single on real grass can easily become a between-the-outfielders triple on synthetic turf if the outfielders aren't quick enough to get to the ball before it skips by them and rolls all the way to the fence.

One of the most unusual outfielders of all time was Pete Gray, who played seventy-seven games for St. Louis in the American League in 1945, during World War II. What made Pete so unusual was that he had only one arm.

Pete Gray at
Yankee Stadium
in 1945

Pete Gray was born in Nanti-
coke, Pennsylvania, in 1917. At
the age of six, he lost his right
arm in an accident. It was ampu-
tated just below the shoulder.
Nevertheless, he was determined
to be a ballplayer, and by perse-
verance and practice he taught
himself to catch, throw, and bat
with only his left arm.

He played in the minor leagues
in 1942, 1943, and 1944, batting
.333 with Memphis in the
Southern Association in 1944 and
handling over 340 chances in the
outfield with only six errors. That
earned him a promotion to the
big leagues.

How did Pete Gray manage to
function in the outfield with
only one arm?

He would catch the ball with
his left (gloved) hand, place the
ball against his chest, let it roll out
of his glove and up his wrist as he
tucked the glove under the stub
of his right arm, and then draw
his left arm back across his chest
until the ball rolled back into his hand. He became so adept at this
maneuver that he could return the ball to the infield almost as
quickly as an ordinary outfielder.

But big league pitching proved too much for him, and he batted only
.218 in seventy-seven games in 1945. He went back to the minors,

where he played until he retired in 1949, at the age of thirty-two. His lifetime minor league batting average was a very respectable .308.

Like infielders, outfielders have to play each batter differently, moving in or out or to one side or the other, depending on who is at bat, who is pitching, what the next pitch is going to be, how the wind is blowing, and so on. Even though it might look like they are just hanging around out there until a ball is hit in their direction, they are alert and thinking on every pitch. (Well, most of them are, anyway.)

Occasionally, however, an outfielder may let his mind wander a bit, especially if he is tired. In 1934, Hack Wilson, the stocky home run hitter (five-foot-six and 195 pounds), was playing right field for the Brooklyn Dodgers. It was a hot, muggy day, and Boom-Boom Beck was pitching for Brooklyn. He wasn't called Boom-Boom for nothing, and on this particular afternoon he was getting hit pretty hard. Line drives were rattling off the tin advertising signs on the right-field wall above Hack's head one after the other, and he was getting exhausted chasing the ball and throwing it back to the infield.

Finally, Casey Stengel, who was managing the Dodgers that year, came out to the mound to change pitchers. Taking advantage of the pause in the game, Hack tried to rest as well as he could out in right field—his hands on his knees, staring down at the grass, trying to catch his breath.

But the unhappy Boom-Boom, instead of handing the ball to Stengel, angrily threw it with all his might out to right field, taking his frustrations out on the baseball.

Hearing the familiar sound of a ball hitting a tin sign above his head, the startled Hack awoke from his daydreams and assumed the game had begun again. As the crowd watched in amusement, he ran after the ball as fast as he could, retrieved it, and fired it on a line to second base, a perfect throw to get the runner—if only there had been one!

360 FEET EQUALS ONE RUN

*A*LL AT ONCE OR A LITTLE AT A TIME? THERE ARE TWO ways to score runs in a ball game. One is by sheer strength, muscling the ball over the fence for a home run. The other is by proceeding less dramatically around the base paths, ninety feet at a time. Either way, 360 feet equals one run, but there's a world of difference between them. In this chapter we are concerned with making it around the bases ninety feet at a time, without benefit of a home run.

In the old days, back when there was only one umpire, a trip from base to base could be quite an adventure. An unsuspecting base runner might be elbowed by the first baseman, given the hip by the second baseman, have his belt grabbed from behind by the shortstop or third baseman, and find home plate blocked by a determined broad-shouldered catcher when he finally got there. Nowadays the journey is much less eventful, but it's still not entirely without its booby traps and minefields.

The first two rules of baserunning are:

(1) *Always know where the ball is.*

(2) *Never trust opposing infielders.*

Think of the embarrassment of a base runner on first base who takes off, head down, at the crack of the bat . . . sees the second baseman or shortstop rush over to second base, glove extended, ready to take a throw . . . and, assuming a close play, slides into second. Only to discover, after the dust has settled, that the batter had hit an easy fly ball to right field and he's already been doubled up by a throw from the right fielder to the first baseman.

Even more embarrassed than a base runner decoyed into sliding into second base is one victimized by the hidden-ball trick. Imagine a base runner starting to take his lead—only to be tagged out suddenly by an infielder who's been nonchalantly standing there with the ball nestled in his glove all the while.

Once big Ernie Lombardi (over six feet tall, 230 pounds) took a lead of a few steps off second base when the opposing second baseman, little Tony Cuccinello (five-foot-seven, 160 pounds), stepped between him and the base, and showed Lombardi what he had in his glove. "You tag me," said Lombardi, "and I'll punch you right in the nose." Needless to say, Cuccinello did not tag him and Ernie just walked off the field back to his dugout.

To repeat: Always know where the ball is and never (ever) trust opposing infielders.

Ever since the first baseball game was played in Hoboken, in 1846, base runners have naturally proceeded in orderly fashion in a counterclockwise direction, from first base to second to third and then home. However, Germany Schaefer, an unconventional utility infielder for the pennant-winning Detroit Tigers in 1907 and 1908, once decided to go the *opposite* way. Detroit outfielder Davy Jones later recalled what happened on that eventful day:

"We were playing Cleveland and the score was tied in a late inning. I was on third base, Schaefer was on first, and before the Cleveland pitcher wound up, Schaefer flashed me the sign for the double steal—meaning he'd take off for second on the next pitch, and when the catcher threw the ball to second I'd take off for home. Well, the pitcher wound up and pitched, and sure enough Schaefer stole second. But I had to stay right where I was, on third, because the Cleveland catcher just held on to the ball; he refused to throw to second, knowing I'd probably score if he did.

"So now we had men on second and third. Well, on the next pitch Schaefer shouted, 'Let's try it again!' And with a bloodcurdling yell he took off *back to first base*, and dove in headfirst in a cloud of dust.

He figured the catcher might throw to first and then I could scoot home, same as before.

"But nothing happened. Nothing at all. Everybody just stood there and watched Schaefer, with their mouths open, not knowing what the devil was going on. Me too. Even if the catcher *had* thrown to first, I was too stunned to move. But the catcher didn't throw. He just stared at this madman running the wrong way on the base path and didn't know *what* to do.

"The umpires were just as confused as everybody else. However, it turned out that there wasn't any rule then against a guy going from second back to first if that's the way he wanted to play baseball, so they had to let it stand.

"So there we were, back where we started, with Schaefer on first and me on third. And on the next pitch darned if he didn't let out another yell and take off *again* for second base. By this time the Cleveland catcher had evidently had enough, because he finally threw to second to get Schaefer, and when he did I took off for home and *both* of us were safe.

"That winter the Rules Committee made it illegal to go the wrong way on the base paths, so that was the one and only time it ever happened."

It's hard to make it all the way around the bases if you can't get to first base to begin with. After all, first is the only base you can't steal. For that reason, many experts believe that lumbering, good-natured Ernie Lombardi, known as the slowest runner of all time, is probably the most underrated hitter in baseball history.

A six-foot-three-inch 230-pounder, Lombardi spent most of his career as a catcher with the Cincinnati Reds in the 1930s. He was about as fast as rush-hour traffic in a snowstorm. When he came to bat, opposing infielders backed up fifteen or twenty feet because that increased the area they could cover, and they knew they had plenty of time to get the ball to first before Ernie would get there. What for

Germany Shaefer:
the only base
runner ever to go
from second base
back to first

Catcher Ernie Lombardi: the slowest runner of all time

most big leaguers was a solid single, even a double, often found Ernie pounding his way down the baseline only to get thrown out at first from somewhere on the outfield grass.

"Lombardi was thrown out at first base," a sportswriter once wrote, "trying to stretch a double into a single."

Nevertheless, he hit over .300 ten times and twice led his league in batting average, something no other catcher has ever done. If Ernie Lombardi could have run with only moderate speed, his name would be listed right up there among the greatest hitters of all time.

Rule (3) *Once you make it to first base, don't let yourself get picked off by the pitcher.*

Easier said than done. Runners on first base all face the same problem. They need to get a decent lead, perhaps to try to steal, but more likely just to get a good jump and avoid a double play in case the batter hits the ball on the ground. And yet the greater the lead, the more likely they'll be picked off by a deceptive pitcher.

Here's a wonderful illustration. In 1974, the Oakland Athletics put twenty-two-year-old Herb Washington, a world-class sprinter, on their roster. He never came to bat or played in the field once all season; his only function was to come in as a pinch runner in late innings, when the game was on the line. Usually he didn't try to steal. What he tried to do was get a good lead, so when the batter hit the ball he could turn on his spectacular speed and avoid a double play or try to score from first on a single.

Washington was one of the fastest short-distance runners in the world, but he was not a baseball player and lacked baseball training. His big moment came in the second game of the 1974 World Series, Oakland vs. the Los Angeles Dodgers, when he was sent to first base as a pinch runner in the ninth inning, representing the potential tying run.

Veteran Los Angeles relief pitcher Mike Marshall made a few easy tosses to first base that led the track star to relax and feel confident about his lead . . . and then the pitcher suddenly whipped the ball over like a flash and caught Washington off base clean as a whistle. Herb Washington is by no means the only one who has been picked off first base, but he is probably the best-known example of the hazards of taking too big a lead.

Base runners prefer to see a right-handed pitcher on the mound, rather than a lefty, because lefties have an advantage in holding base runners close to first base. Since a left-handed pitcher is facing first base when he takes his pitching position, it is easier for him to keep a man on first from taking too big a lead than it is for a right-handed pitcher, who is facing in the opposite direction.

Sam Jones, a star pitcher in the American League from 1914 to 1935, attributed his long career to the fact that he *rarely* threw to first base to hold base runners close. He claimed that there were only so many pitches in his arm, and he didn't believe in wasting them by throwing to first base.

"What you do instead of throwing," he later told a friend, "is look at the guy on first base. That's all, just stand there on the pitching mound and look at him. There's no need to throw. If you stare at him long enough, it'll get to be too much for him, and he'll lean back toward the base. Then you pitch. There was a time there, for five years, I never once threw to first base to chase a runner back. Not one time in five years. Then one day, to everybody's surprise, I did it. I threw to first base. Had the guy out by a mile. But it didn't do any good. The man was safe because my first baseman was as surprised as anyone—so surprised that he *dropped the ball!*"

Ivan "Pudge" Rodriguez is a strong hitter—plus he's generally considered the best defensive catcher of the 1990s.

Rule (4) *Be sure to touch all the bases.*

When Casey Stengel was managing the New York Mets in the 1960s, he had a big first baseman named Marvelous Marv Throneberry, who seemed to personify all the troubles the Mets had in those days. In one game Marvelous Marv hit two triples and both times was called out by the umpires for failing to touch second base. The second time it happened Manager Stengel rushed out of the dugout to protest, but before he got to the foul line his first-base coach stopped him: "Don't bother, Casey," he said. "He didn't touch first base either."

* * *

Baserunning and base *stealing*, by the way, are two quite different skills. It is true that superb base stealers—like Ty Cobb, Maury Wills, Lou Brock, and Rickey Henderson—were also excellent base runners. However, there have been many good base stealers who were much less skillful when it came to running the bases. By the same token, many outstanding base runners did very little base stealing.

For example, Baltimore third baseman Brooks Robinson hardly ever stole a base, but his manager, Earl Weaver, admiringly observed that "he always seems to know if he should go from first to third on a single to right, or if he can score from second on a base hit."

Similarly, Mickey Mantle and Joe DiMaggio were first-rate base *runners*, but they stole few bases. Mantle averaged less than ten stolen bases a season, DiMaggio only two or three. Nevertheless, both of them were considered superb base runners.

Mantle and DiMaggio turned ordinary singles into doubles, and doubles into triples, and when on base they instinctively knew how far they could advance on a teammate's hit. By quickly evaluating the outfielder's arm, the force and direction of the wind, the stage of the ball game, the element of surprise, and a host of other variables, they were able to make the most of every baserunning opportunity and were rarely thrown out. On similar plays, faster runners who stole more bases would be thrown out more often, because their baserunning judgment was not as good.

Base *stealing* requires the ability to "read" pitchers (to know when they are going to throw to first base or to home plate), the ability to accelerate rapidly from a standing start, and sheer speed. Baserunning is facilitated by speed, but even more important is the ability to take into account a large number of variables and quickly assess their implications for reaching the next base or beyond.

One of the most dramatic baserunning episodes in baseball history took place in 1946: it was Enos Slaughter's explosive race, to score successfully from first base on a single, in the deciding game of the

Enos Slaughter slides across home plate as he scores from first base in the 1946 World Series.

1946 World Series (Cardinals vs. Red Sox). Slaughter, right fielder for the Cardinals, was on first base with the score tied and two outs late in the seventh game of the Series, when teammate Harry Walker hit a line drive over the head of Red Sox shortstop Johnny Pesky into center field.

Pesky rushed out to take the relay from the center fielder and whirled around to throw to third base, where he expected Slaughter to be. Instead of stopping at the base, though, as everyone thought he would, Slaughter rounded third at full throttle and flew toward home plate. Pesky hesitated a split second—perhaps a fatal moment—and then threw home, but Slaughter arrived ahead of the ball and slid across the plate safely.

The official scorer gave Harry Walker a double, but it was really a single with the batter taking second on the throw home. In any event, Enos Slaughter, who averaged only three or four stolen bases a year over a nineteen-year career, demonstrated conclusively why base stealing and baserunning are two rather different skills.

On the subject of base stealing, one topic that always starts an argument is whether it is easier to steal second or third base. Most people assume it is easier to steal second because the catcher has such a long throw to make: it is slightly over 127 feet from home plate to second base and only ninety feet from home to third base.

However, many expert base stealers claim that in fact it is easier to steal third. A base runner on second base can get a longer lead than one on first base—perhaps about fifteen feet as compared with a lead of only five feet or so from first base—because it is so much more difficult for a pitcher to pick a runner off second than off first. In addition, most batters are right-handed. Their batter's box is on the third base side of home plate, so they partially block the catcher when he has to throw to third base.

The reason steals of third base are not attempted as often as steals of second, even though they may be easier, is because a base runner on second base is already considered to be in "scoring position"—that is, he is likely to make it home on a solid single. Most managers believe that to take a chance on being thrown out trying to steal third, when a player is *already* in scoring position, involves too large a potential cost relative to the potential gain.

A bizarre baserunning event took place in Oxnard, California, in 1913. At that time, third baseman Hans Lobert of the Philadelphia Phillies was the fastest man in the game at circling the bases. He held the record of 13.8 seconds around the bases from home to home.

Following an exhibition game in Oxnard, Lobert agreed to race a horse around the bases. Let him tell you what happened:

"As soon as the ball game ended, out from this mass of cowboys encircling the outfield stepped the most beautiful black animal you ever saw, with a Mexican cowboy on him all dressed up in chaps and spangles. Both he and the horse were glittering like jewels in the sunlight. The horse was a beautiful coal-black pony that was trained to herd cows and so was used to making sharp turns.

"The cowboy couldn't speak English, so I said, 'Señor, practico. Let's take a practice walk around the bases.'

"So around we walked, with the crowd roaring. I was supposed to touch the inner corner of each base, and he was to go around the outside, so as not to run me down.

"Finally, everything was all set. Bill Klem, the National League umpire, was the referee. A pistol started us, and off we went. I led at first base by at least five feet, and by second base I had picked up and was at least ten feet ahead. I was in perfect stride, hitting the inside corner of each bag with my right foot and going faster all the time.

"But instead of the horse keeping his distance, he crowded me between second and third and I had to dodge to avoid being knocked down. I broke stride, and that was the end. I was still in front as we rounded third, but not by much, and on the home stretch the horse just did beat me in. I still think I would have won if I hadn't been practically bowled over at shortstop."

Rule (5) *Beware of base runners ahead of you and don't catch up with or pass them.*
The most glaring example of what can happen when rule five is not taken to heart occurred in a Brooklyn Dodgers-Boston Braves game in Brooklyn's Ebbets Field on August 15, 1926. Brooklyn loaded the bases with the score tied and one out in the seventh inning: The Brooklyn catcher was on third base, the Dodger pitcher (Dazzy Vance) on second base, and Brooklyn infielder Chick Fewster on first base.

Up to the plate came the Babe—not Babe Ruth, but Brooklyn's Babe, Babe Herman, a mighty slugger in his own right. Herman promptly walloped a long drive to right; it was hard to say whether it would be caught or would hit the wall. In fact, it hit the wall, and the man on third scored easily. Vance held up so long on second, waiting to see if the ball would be caught, that he could only make it halfway to home—so at the last minute he decided to play it safe and scampered back to third. Chick Fewster kept on going from first and made it to third, so that as Vance came back to third Fewster was already there, standing on the base.

And Babe Herman just kept on going as fast as he could, without looking up at anything. So as Vance slid back to third, and Fewster stood on the base, Herman slid into third from the second-base side. It's a wonder Fewster didn't get spiked.

The third baseman didn't know what to do, so he tagged all of them. The umpires finally declared that Fewster and Herman were out, which ended the inning.

Three men on third! With the passage of time, the Three Stooges scene took on a life of its own and people started to believe that Herman had tripled into a triple play! But he couldn't have done that, because there was one out to begin with. Trying to set the record straight, one sportswriter summed it up by writing, "Babe Herman never tripled into a triple play, but he did double into a double play, which is the next best thing."

The incident inspired jokes about the Brooklyn Dodgers that continued long after the Dodgers had departed from Brooklyn. Such as the one about the taxicab that is cruising past Ebbets Field and the cabdriver sticks his head out of the window and yells up at a spectator, "How's the game going?"

"The Dodgers have three men on base," a fan shouts back.

"Which base?" the driver asks.

How to Be a Big League Manager in One Easy Lesson

BASEBALL GAMES ARE FUN TO WATCH BECAUSE you're rooting for your team to win. A home run by your team is great, and one by the other team is terrible. But, in addition, a lot of other things are happening that are also fun to know about. Once you become familiar with them, you'll enjoy the game even more (provided, of course, that your team wins).

Take the batting order, for instance. Once the manager hands it to the home-plate umpire, right before the game starts, it's fixed for that game and can't be changed. Substitutions can he made, but the substitutes have to replace someone in the original batting order and bat in that person's place. And once a player has been taken out of a game, he cannot play again in that particular game.

The manager doesn't make out his batting order by pulling numbers out of a hat. He has nine players—ten if there is a designated hitter, who bats in place of the pitcher—and he wants to have them coming to bat in a sequence that he figures will produce the most runs.

The leadoff man, the first man up in the batting order, is usually the team's fastest runner. His job is to get on base any way he can as often as possible. He's likely to be a singles-type hitter who coaxes a lot of bases on balls, bunts frequently, and once he gets on first base will be a threat to steal second. Three of the greatest base stealers of all time—Rickey Henderson, Lou Brock, and Maury Wills—all batted leadoff, for example.

Second place in the batting order is usually reserved for the team's best place hitter. Typically, he's a good hitter who doesn't strike out often. The first and second men in the batting order will tend to score a lot of runs (hopefully), but they won't rank very high in runs batted in, because they have less opportunity to drive in runs than those who follow them.

Third, fourth, and fifth are the power hitters, the big men who are capable of hitting the ball over the fence. They are relied on to drive in the runs. The number-three batter is often the team's best hitter in terms of batting average and power, while the fourth and fifth are more strictly power oriented. Babe Ruth and Roberto Clemente usually batted third. Ken Griffey, Jr., also generally bats third in the batting order, as does Mark McGwire, while Sammy Sosa usually bats fourth.

It is impossible to generalize on this, however, because Joe DiMaggio almost always batted fourth, in what has traditionally been called the "cleanup" spot. Many power hitters consider it an honor to be the cleanup batter, with special responsibility for clearing the bases and driving in runs. Historically, though, just as many great hitters have batted third in the batting order as fourth.

The sixth through ninth places are always filled by the weaker hitters. This is so if only because the higher a player is in the batting order, the more times he will come to bat in a game. During the course of an entire season, the top half of the batting order will come to bat over a hundred times more than the bottom half. A manager wants his best hitters to have the most chances to hit.

Other factors also have to be taken into account. For example, if the opposing pitcher is a lefty, then it is better to have right-handed batters facing him. Remember: Left-handed batters hit righties best, while right-handed batters hit lefties best. Many managers alternate (or platoon) two players at one or more positions, starting the right-handed batter when the opposing pitcher is a lefty and starting the left-handed batter when the opposing pitcher is a righty.

Nowadays many managers use computer calculations in making out their batting order as well as in making other decisions before

Casey Stengel won seven World Series as manager of the Yankees—but as manager of the expansion Mets from 1962 to 1965, he finished last every year.

and during a game. Computer printouts show, among other things, how certain batters have performed against particular pitchers and how certain pitchers have done in various game situations. Other managers rely more on their personal experience—that is, mainly on hunches and psychological insights in making their decisions. Whether one method is better than another is an open question. In all probability, a combination of computer analyses *and* personal experience is probably optimum.

Once a batter makes it to first base, of course, the idea is to get him all the way around the bases to score a run. It's runs that are important, not hits. If a team has a lot of good power hitters, the manager is likely to play it safe and just wait for a big hit to drive a base runner in.

But if a team is short on good power hitters, or if they strike out too much, other strategies may be necessary. A favorite is the famous *hit-and-run play*, which is intended to move a runner from first base all the way to third on a single.

With the hit-and-run play, the man on first base takes off for second as soon as the pitcher starts to throw the ball toward home plate. Thinking the base runner is trying to steal second, the second baseman (or the shortstop) dashes over to second base to take the throw from the catcher. The batter's job is to then hit the ball through the part of the infield just vacated by the second baseman (or the shortstop). It really should be called the run-and-hit play rather than the hit-and-run, because the base runner starts running before the batter hits the ball.

The batter's chances of hitting safely are increased because the second baseman (or the shortstop) has left his normal defensive position unguarded. And if the batter does get a hit, the man on first base should easily make it all the way around to third on a single because he has had such a big head start.

The hit-and-run is also helpful in keeping the batter from hitting into a double play on a ground ball. Nothing takes the steam out of a rally faster than someone hitting into a double play. Since the man on first is already well on his way to second base by the time the ball is hit, he's likely to get there safely even if the batter hits a hard ground ball directly at an infielder—a grounder that, with a man on first, would normally result in a double play.

If the hit-and-run is such a great play, then why isn't it used all the time? Because there are risks involved in using it. Unless the batter is a really good place hitter who can hit the ball *on the ground*, it's a dangerous play.

If the batter hits a line drive at an infielder or a not very high pop-up, the hit-and-run backfires and becomes a sure double play. After catching it, the infielder can easily throw to first for a double play before the runner can get back. If the batter misses the ball entirely or fails to swing, perhaps because he missed a sign, the catcher can throw the runner out at second.

Indeed, if the catcher anticipates that a hit-and-run play is coming up, he'll signal the pitcher to throw a *pitchout*—a pitch that comes in shoulder high and a few feet wide of home plate, where the batter can't reach it—and then the catcher can easily throw the surprised runner out at second. Pitchouts are deliberately thrown so batters can't reach them, but every once in a while an intended pitchout comes a little too close to the plate and then the happy batter can jump on it for a solid base hit.

It is obvious that signs from the manager to the players are very important on the hit-and-run play and on all other special plays as well. Both the batter and the base runner have to know that the play is "on" for the next pitch. A story is often told about a major league batter who failed to swing at a pitch under such circumstances, so that the man on first was easily thrown out at second.

In this case, the manager's signals were based on giving number values to a few simple signs—like "three" for the manager taking his hat off and "four" for crossing his legs. Players were supposed to add up the numbers to determine what to do. When the batter came back to the bench, the manager asked him, "Didn't you see me take my hat off *and* cross my legs?"

"Of course," said the player.

"Don't you know that a total of seven means that you're supposed to swing at the pitch?"

"Sure," said the player.

"Then why the heck didn't you swing?"

Shortstop Nomar Garciaparra is a powerful hitter and a slick fielder. The shortstops of the '90s are, as a group, the best in baseball history.

Frank Thomas, the American League's MVP in 1993 and 1994

"I didn't know I was supposed to" was the player's response. "Doesn't three plus four add up to eight?"

Another popular strategy to advance a runner from first base is the *sacrifice bunt*. With a man on first base and fewer than two men out, the manager tells the batter to sacrifice the base runner to second. It's called a sacrifice because what the batter does is "sacrifice" himself, or give up his own chance to get a hit, in order to move the runner from first to second base for the good of the team.

The batter does this by bunting the ball *on the ground* so it rolls twenty-five or thirty feet into the infield. He is usually thrown out at first, but by that time the runner has moved to second, where he is now in scoring position—that is, where he has a good chance of scoring even on a single.

Not all bunts are sacrifices. Often a batter who is fast will bunt to try to get on first base. The difference between bunting for a hit and a sacrifice bunt is that the main idea of a sacrifice bunt is to move the base runner to the next base. It is *expected* that the batter will be thrown out at first.

Sometimes when a batter lays down a good sacrifice bunt and gets thrown out at first base, the fans give him a big hand as he trots back to the dugout. Others wonder why all the applause—after all, he's out, isn't he? The reason for the applause is that he's done his job and done it well: he's advanced the runner to the next base, which is exactly what he was supposed to do.

There are two problems with a sacrifice bunt. The first is that it automatically gives up an out unless an infielder makes an error. Outs are precious because it takes only three of them to retire the side.

The second problem is that very few ballplayers are good bunters nowadays. They either bunt the ball too hard and too far, resulting in a double play, or they pop it up in the air and it is caught as a fly ball, with the runner unable to advance. More close games are lost in the late innings because of failures to sacrifice successfully than for any other reason.

One special bunting situation, and one of the most exciting plays in baseball, is called the *squeeze play*. With a man on third base and less than two out, the batter bunts the ball on the ground, and the base runner takes off and tries to score on the bunt. The squeeze play has two forms: the suicide squeeze and the safety squeeze.

With the *suicide squeeze*, the man on third starts running for home as soon as the pitcher throws the ball. If the batter makes any kind of decent bunt at all—that is, if he doesn't pop the ball up in the air or miss it completely—the base runner is almost certain to slide across home plate safely. On the other hand, if the batter fails to bunt the ball—if he pops it up or misses it, perhaps because the catcher called for a pitchout—then the base runner is a sure out.

With the *safety squeeze*, the man on third base is more cautious. He waits until he sees the batter actually bunt the ball on the ground, and then he takes off for home. It's less risky than the suicide squeeze, but the bunt has to be better (or the base runner faster) because the base runner has gotten a later start. Both squeeze plays are exciting, but neither one is seen very often because so few batters can be counted on to bunt well.

The reason that bunting is a lost art is because nowadays the major

After five years with the Baltimore Orioles, Rafael Palmiero returned to his previous team, the Texas Rangers, in the 1998 off-season.

emphasis in baseball is on hitting for distance, on driving the ball over the fence. Home runs are more glamorous than bunts, and players who can launch a baseball four hundred feet usually get fatter paychecks than players who are skillful at pushing it a mere fifteen or twenty feet. Indeed, it's been that way ever since a young man named George Herman Ruth revolutionized the game way back in 1920. It was outfielder Ralph Kiner, a noted home run hitter himself in the forties and fifties, who put it in a nutshell: "Home run hitters," he said, "drive Cadillacs. Singles hitters drive Fords."

The hit-and-run, sacrifice bunt, and squeeze play are all *offensive* plays. Their purpose is to help score runs. But managers also spend a lot of time thinking about *defensive* strategy—how to stop the other team from scoring.

The pitchout, for example, is a defensive maneuver. When the manager of the team in the field anticipates a hit-and-run play by the team up at bat or an attempt to steal a base, he can signal for a pitchout. This enables the catcher to throw the base runner out and spoil a potential rally.

One defensive tactic that always gets boos from fans of the team up at bat is an *intentional walk*. The pitcher throws four balls in a row, each well wide of the plate, and the batter trots to first base. Why would a manager ever tell his pitcher to walk an opposing batter on purpose?

One possible reason is that the batter is so dangerous the manager would rather pitch to the next man in the batting order. It's no accident that the all-time leaders in bases on balls are Babe Ruth and Ted Williams.

Just as often, however, it is done because base runners are already on second and third and first base is open. The manager *wants* to load the bases because that sets up the possibility of a defensive play—*a force-out at any base*—that is not possible unless first base is occupied. With the bases full, all base runners are forced to run when the batter hits a ground ball because two men can't be on one base at the same time—they have to run to make room for the advancing base runners behind them.

Philadelphia manager Connie Mack is offered a flower by a young admirer in exchange for an autographed baseball. Slugger Jimmie Foxx is obviously intrigued.

This means that a base runner can now be forced out by an infielder fielding a ground ball and just stepping on any base, including home plate, before the runner gets there. If this sounds complicated, remember that it happens all the time with the familiar second-base-to-first-base double play, where the shortstop or second baseman only has to touch second to force out the runner coming down from first. The runner is forced out because the batter who hit the ground ball is advancing to take over first base.

When first base is unoccupied, on the other hand, no force-out is possible. If the batter hits a ground ball, the base runners on second and third can simply stay put if they want to.

It is also easier to make a double play when the bases are filled than when runners are only on second and third. With the bases loaded, an infielder with the ball can step on *any* base to force a runner and then throw to first base to get the batter. Again, if first base had been unoccupied, no force-out would have been possible anywhere.

For these reasons, if base runners are already on second and third, it often makes sense to deliberately walk the batter and put someone on first base, too. This is especially true if the batter is a dangerous hitter and it is late in the game. You can still boo if the opposing manager does it to your favorite home-run slugger, but now you'll understand why he's doing it.

Of course, like all strategies, both offensive and defensive, it doesn't always work. If the next batter hits a home run with the bases loaded, the manager doesn't look too smart. Babe Ruth was followed in the New York Yankee batting order by Lou Gehrig, and many times the Babe was intentionally walked when men were already on second and third. It probably worked some of the time but not all of the time: Lou Gehrig hit an all-time record twenty-three home runs with the bases loaded!

There have been many famous managers in baseball history—Connie Mack, John McGraw, Frank Chance, and Casey Stengel, to name but four. All of them had losing as well as winning years.

Connie Mack managed the Philadelphia Athletics for fifty years, from 1901 through 1950. When he retired, in 1950, he was eighty-seven years old. A catcher in his playing days, Connie won nine pennants and five World Series, but he also finished last in the American League *seventeen* times. How could he remain as manager so long if he finished last so many times? It's simple: He owned the team.

John J. McGraw managed the New York Giants from 1902 to 1932.

He won ten pennants and three World Series, and finished last in the National League twice. A scrappy manager who previously had been an outstanding third baseman, he believed in bunting, place hitting, and stealing bases. He could never adapt to the lively ball and the home-run hitting it stimulated. When Babe Ruth was still a pitcher but playing in the outfield occasionally as well, McGraw's only comment about Ruth was "If he plays every day, the bum will hit into a hundred double plays a season."

Frank Chance was player-manager of the pennant-winning Chicago Cubs in 1906, 1907, 1908, and 1910. He was the first baseman of the famous Tinker to Evers to Chance double-play combination of those years. As manager of the Cubs and later of the Yankees and Red Sox, he won four pennants and two World Series and also finished last once.

Casey Stengel knew both the highs and the lows. He won ten pennants and seven World Series as manager of the New York Yankees, including a record five World Series in a row from 1949 through 1953. But as manager of the New York Mets from 1962 to 1965, he finished last every year.

Everything considered, how important is a manager to the success of a baseball team?

Listen to Lefty O'Doul, a great hitter in the 1920s and early 1930s, who had a .349 lifetime batting average. "I played for a lot of managers in my day," he once said, "including John McGraw, Frank Chance, and Miss Rosie Stultz. The most successful of all was Rosie Stultz. She was our seventh-grade teacher at Bay View Grammar School, and she managed the school team. We won the grade-school championship of San Francisco in 1912 with Miss Rosie Stultz managing.

"A manager can only do so much," O'Doul continued. "The rest is up to the players. It's the players who make the manager, not the other way around. I managed for twenty-four years myself in the minor leagues, in the Pacific Coast League. In 1935, I had Joe

DiMaggio playing in the outfield and won the pennant. He hit .398. He was sold to the Yankees that winter, and the next year I finished next to last. Do you want another example? Take Frank Chance. He was one of the greatest, right? He won all those pennants with the Chicago Cubs. Well, Frank Chance was my manager on the Boston Red Sox in 1923, and where do you think we finished? Dead last, that's where.

"Which just goes to prove," O'Doul concluded, "if you haven't got the players, you haven't got a chance!"

SIGNS AND SIGNALS

BASEBALL'S SECRET LANGUAGE

*M*YSTERIES ARE FUN, AND AMONG THE MOST mysterious aspects of baseball are all those crazy gyrations that the third-base coach is always performing—like touching different parts of his uniform, from the bill of his cap to the letters on his shirt; pulling on his left earlobe; popping his gum; and who knows what else.

What he's doing is communicating in baseball language with a batter or base runner: Specifically, he's telling them to bunt or to steal or something of that sort. The message has to be secret because if the opposition catches on they'll retaliate appropriately. For example, if the opposing pitcher learns that the "steal" sign is on, the pitcher will respond with a pitchout and the base runner will be thrown out easily.

The third-base coach isn't the only one who gives signs and signals. (Players consider the words *signs* and *signals* synonyms and use them interchangeably.) In addition to the third-base coach, the catcher gives signs to the pitcher, the manager gives signs to the third-base coach and others, infielders give signs to each other and to outfielders, and sometimes outfielders even give signs to catchers. Let's look at each in turn.

As we know from earlier chapters, the catcher is the defensive team leader on the field. With hand signals, he "calls" the pitches that the pitcher throws—the usual signals are one finger for a fastball, two for a curve, three a change of pace, and four a special pitch (like a screwball). Sometimes the last two are reversed, with three fingers meaning a special pitch and four a change of pace.

The catcher also often indicates the location of the pitch—

whether it should be thrown on the inside or outside of the plate—by touching his left or right inner thigh while he is still down in his crouch. In addition, variations on these themes can indicate whether a pitch is to be thrown high or low, when a pitchout is wanted, and when a pitcher should throw to a base in hopes of picking off a careless base runner.

At times the catcher is just an intermediary, passing along orders from the manager. That is, the manager, from the dugout, tells the catcher what to call for. Some managers do this all the time, while others do it occasionally or only with a rookie catcher who hasn't yet had time to become familiar with opposing batters or with the strengths and weaknesses of his own pitchers. The manager might touch the bill of his cap for a fastball or touch his elbow for a curve, or something like that, and then the catcher will transmit the instructions to the pitcher via his usual hand signals.

If the pitcher disagrees and wants to throw a different pitch, he either shakes his head or wiggles his glove or perhaps rubs his glove across his shirt. Since batters usually try to anticipate what kind of pitch is coming, pitchers sometimes shake off their catcher not because they really disagree but just to confuse the batter. The pitcher might eventually throw the same pitch the catcher first called for, but by then the batter has had second thoughts.

The story is often told of a rookie pitcher on the mound in a close game with the bases loaded and Hank Aaron up at bat. The catcher put down one finger for a fastball, only to have the young pitcher shake his head. The catcher put down two fingers for a curve, but the pitcher shook his head again. Three fingers for a change of pace, followed by another shake of the head. Disgusted, the catcher called time and trotted out for a face-to-face conference on the mound. "What's going on?" he asked. "I've called every pitch I can think of and you keep shaking me off. What do you want to do, anyway?"

"I don't want to do anything," the pitcher answered. "I just want to hold the ball as long as I can."

Catchers Mike
Piazza (left) and
Sandy Alomar, Jr.,
are team leaders.

* * *

Signs to batters and base runners—such as to bunt or steal or hit-and-run—usually originate with the manager. He signals one of his coaches, usually the third-base coach, who relays the instructions to the batter and/or base runners.

That's why you frequently see a batter take a long hard look toward third base before getting set in the batter's box. He wants to know from the coach if it's okay to swing away for a base hit or if he has some special orders: For instance, is he supposed to sacrifice bunt or hit-and-run or "take" a pitch? Taking a pitch means not swinging at it, just letting the pitch go by; a manager might want a batter to take the next pitch, for example, when the count is 3 balls and 0 strikes, hoping for ball four and a free ticket to first base.

For each sign, the coach goes through an elaborate routine, touching various parts of his body in different sequences as he transmits instructions to the batter and/or base runner. Most of the routine is camouflage, designed to deceive the opposition so they can't figure out what's happening.

As an illustration, the third-base coach might make a number of motions but none of them means anything until he touches his belt buckle. In this case his belt buckle is called the "indicator"—which means from now on, no more make-believe. Thereafter, when he touches his nose or the bill of his cap it might mean hit-and-run or bunt or whatever. But touching his nose or the bill of his cap means nothing until it is preceded by that belt buckle!

Signs weren't always so complicated. In the early 1900s Luther "Dummy" Taylor, a deaf mute, was one of the New York Giants' best pitchers. In order to make sure he was a full-fledged member of the team, socially as well as on the playing field, Manager John McGraw had all the Giants learn sign language, which he then used for many of his signals. McGraw frequently coached at third base, and there he would give the signals by spelling out S-T-E-A-L or B-U-N-T with his fingers, plain as the nose on your face to anyone in the ballpark who could read sign language.

As a matter of fact, another deaf mute, Bill "Dummy" Hoy, an out-fielder who played way back in the 1880s, was responsible for the hand signs that umpires still give for balls and strikes—raising the right hand to indicate a strike and showing the count (that is, the number of balls and strikes) with the fingers of the left hand for balls and the right hand for strikes. Dummy Hoy would be up at bat and he couldn't hear and couldn't talk. He'd look around at the umpire to see what the pitch was, a ball or a strike, and the umpire would respond with hand signs that soon became standard. Eventually, all the umpires used them regardless of who was at bat.

All signs are important, but some are more important than others. Perhaps most important of all is the sign for a suicide squeeze play when a right-handed batter is at bat. On a squeeze play, remember, the batter bunts the ball and the base runner on third base takes off for home plate. When it's a *suicide* squeeze, the man on third doesn't wait for the bunt—he starts running as soon as the pitcher releases the ball.

If a right-handed batter misses the sign on this play, somebody could get hurt. If he misses the sign and just lets the pitch go by, he's going to be awfully surprised to hear the pounding feet of his own teammate getting close enough to climb right up his back. Or if he swings and hits a line drive down the third-base line, he could prac-tically tear the head off the astonished base runner, who'll be halfway to home by then.

If a left-handed batter misses the sign on a suicide squeeze play, at least he's facing third base and will see that *something* is going on, so he'll be able to get out of the way without making matters worse.

Yankee manager Casey Stengel, who won five American League pennants and World Series in a row, used to complain that some ballplayers tried to think too much for their own good. "You fellows do the hitting and fielding," he'd say, "and leave the thinking to me." To illustrate his point, he liked to tell about a batter who was given the bunt sign but, instead of trying to bunt, just stood there and never moved a muscle. As a result, the base runner on first base was easily thrown out at second.

When the young man returned to the bench after striking out, Casey asked him, very patiently, "Do you know that when I scratch my nose, that's the bunt sign?"

"Yes, sir," said the player.

"Did you see me scratching my nose?" Casey asked.

"Yes, sir," said the player.

"Then why didn't you try to bunt the ball?"

"I didn't think you really meant it," the player answered.

Sometimes coaches try to do away with movement signs and replace them with verbal signs. However, verbal signs don't work too well because the roar of the crowd, especially at crucial moments in a game, can drown out whatever the coach is trying to say. Also they are liable to be misunderstood, like the third-base coach who yelled "Whoa!" to an approaching base runner only to see him round the bag like a scared rabbit and continue on toward home—where he was thrown out by a mile.

"Didn't you hear me say 'Whoa'?" the coach asked him later.

"I thought you said 'Go'!" explained the embarrassed base runner.

Aside from the catcher's signals to the pitcher, so far we've been discussing *offensive* signs. Bunting, hit-and-run, and steal signs, for instance, are all concerned with offensive tactics. There are also *defensive* signs, although they are much less well known. One defensive sign that is flashed many times during a typical game, but that hardly any spectators are aware of, is communication between the shortstop and second baseman whenever a base runner gets on first base and second base is unoccupied. The shortstop and second baseman have to decide in advance who will cover second base and take the throw from the catcher, in case the man on first should try to steal second.

Otherwise, neither one may cover second and the catcher's throw

Chan Ho Park is one of the many foreign-born players who starred in the majors in the '90s.

will sail past the base and into center field. Or they may *both* run over to take the throw and crash right into each other.

To prevent either of these Laurel and Hardy scenes, the shortstop and second baseman exchange signs before every pitch, specifying who will cover in case of an attempted steal. Usually the shortstop gives the sign, and traditionally it is a quick open mouth or closed mouth, concealed from general view by the shortstop's glove. Open mouth (as in *you*) means the second baseman should cover, while closed mouth (like the *m* in *me*) indicates the shortstop will take the throw. Generally, the shortstop covers when the batter is left-handed and the second baseman when the batter is right-handed.

This action can usually be seen only if you're watching at the ballpark, since television cameras rarely focus on the shortstop and second baseman before a pitch. Unfortunately, most spectators at the game miss it too, since they almost always look at the pitcher or batter before a pitch, or possibly at a base runner taking a lead, but hardly ever at the shortstop and second baseman. The next time you're at a game and a man gets on first, with second base empty, try dragging your attention away from the pitcher and batter and watch the interaction between the shortstop and second baseman as they await the next pitch.

On the other hand, being at the game makes it virtually impossible to see the catcher's signs to the pitcher. Only fans in the center field stands are in any position to see these, and unless they have powerful binoculars they are too far away. The catcher's signals can be seen perfectly on television, however, because the center field camera often zooms in for close-ups of his finger movements. For the most part, baseball is more fun at the ballpark, but in this one respect it is better on television.

Infielders also signal to outfielders as well as to each other. Outfielders are too far away to see the catcher's signs, so they rely on signals from the shortstop and second baseman to tell them whether the next pitch will be a fastball or a curve. Infielders give such signs to outfielders with hand signals behind their back—usually closed fist for a fastball and open hand for a curve, sometimes one finger for a fastball, two for a curve.

Why do outfielders care whether the next pitch is a fastball or a curve? Because the kind of pitch will influence *where* the batter may hit the ball, providing he hits it at all. The faster the pitch, the less likely a batter will be able to get his bat around quickly enough to "pull" the ball—that is, hit it with his full strength and power. Right-handed batters naturally "pull" the ball toward left field, while left-handed hitters naturally "pull" it toward right field. (Home-run hitters are primarily pull hitters, by the way, while place hitters are not.)

A center fielder who sees a right-handed batter at the plate and knows that the next pitch will be a fastball is likely to shift a few steps toward right field, figuring the batter (a righty) will not pull the ball (toward left field). On the other hand, if he knows that a change-of-pace pitch is coming up, he realizes the batter has a better chance to pull the ball, so he'll shift a few paces toward left field.

On rare occasions outfielders have even given signals. For example, when Frank Robinson was playing right field for the Baltimore Orioles he managed to decipher the Yankees' hit-and-run sign from Yankee manager Ralph Houk's movements. Houk had a habit of sitting on the top step of the Yankee dugout, in full view of everyone, where he absentmindedly tossed pebbles during the game. From his position in right field, Robinson could watch Houk's every move; whenever Robinson saw Houk give the hit-and-run sign, he'd quickly flash a sign of his own to the Baltimore catcher—who would of course call for a pitchout and nab the base runner.

Ah, sign stealing! The subject has intrigued major leaguers for well over a century. Almost every team has at least one sign-stealing expert who specializes in decoding the enemy's secret messages. After their playing careers have ended, many of these experts become coaches—usually third-base coaches, as a matter of fact. When their own team is at bat, they wiggle and waggle in the third-base coach's box, but when the other team comes to bat, they concentrate on trying to decipher the instructions the other third-base coach is signaling.

Often two or three second-string players, who are usually on the bench when their opponents are at bat, will put their heads together and try to figure out the other team's signals. For the hit-and-run or steal sign, for instance, one will watch the opposing manager, one the third-base coach, and one the base runner. The sign stealers will then say out loud what each of them is doing and try to find sequences that reveal the meaning of the signs. Their commentary might run something like this:

"He's rubbing his nose," says the one watching the manager.

"He's touching the bill of his cap," says the one covering the third-base coach.

"Forget the whole thing," says the one watching the base runner. "He's looking in the stands trying to find his girlfriend."

Al Schacht (at left) and Nick Altrock (wearing a fashionable hat) were the third- and first-base coaches, respectively, for the old Washington Senators. Their pregame antics drew as many fans to the ballpark as the game itself.

Catcher-to-pitcher hand signals are sometimes read by opposing coaches because catchers fail to hide their signs effectively. The coach will read the sign right along with the pitcher and let the batter know what's coming. Pitchers themselves might tip off what they are going to throw by some unconscious mannerism.

When Babe Ruth was a young pitcher, for example, he acquired the habit of curling his tongue in the corner of his mouth when throwing his curveball. He didn't break the habit, he recalled years later, "until Bill Carrigan, my first big league manager, convinced me that I was 'telegraphing' every curve with my tongue."

Hank Greenberg, the great homer-hitting first baseman for the Detroit Tigers in the thirties and forties, hit .340 with forty-one homers and 150 runs batted in for the pennant-winning Tigers in 1940. "I knew what was coming all year," he said later. "Our manager, Del Baker, was also our third-base coach, and he was a genius at reading a catcher's signs or picking up on a pitcher's mannerisms. If he yelled 'All right' when I was at bat, that meant the next pitch was going to be a fastball. If he said 'Come on,' that meant a curve. Like 'All right, Hank, you can do it,' would tell me a fastball was on its way. 'Come on, Hank, you can do it,' meant a curve was coming.

"I was having such a great year that around midseason Baker started thinking it was all his doing. He started taking credit for my hitting. At one point it seemed as though if he called a pitch correctly and I hit a home run, he thought it was *his* home run. That man was a real good sign stealer, no doubt about it, but there's a big difference between *knowing* what's coming and *hitting* it!"

Some batters don't want to know what's coming, because if the coach makes a mistake it could be dangerous. Say a coach tells a right-handed batter that a right-handed pitcher is going to throw a curveball on the next pitch. The batter sees the ball coming at him but doesn't try to get out of the way because he assumes the pitch is going to curve away from him at the last second. If the coach is wrong, however, and it is in fact a fastball, the batter could find himself not on the way to first base but on the way to the hospital.

Not all sign stealing is as innocent and as legitimate as the examples already mentioned. The Chicago White Sox once bought a World War II submarine periscope from war surplus and put it in their center-field scoreboard. From there, someone could see the opposing catcher's signs and let the home-team batter know what was coming.

Even earlier, the Philadelphia Athletics had someone with binoculars sitting on a rooftop across the street from the ballpark. From his perch, the observer could see the catcher's signals at least as well as the pitcher. He relayed the signals by turning a large weather vane on the rooftop in different positions, according to the upcoming pitch. His credibility was called into question, however, when he failed to notice that the wind often moved the weather vane without any reference whatsoever to fastballs or curves!

BASEBALL CARDS AND AUTOGRAPHS

BEWARE OF COUNTERFEITS AND FORGERIES

*B*ASEBALL CARDS ARE PRACTICALLY AS OLD AS THE game itself. They used to be called "trading" cards because kids collected them and traded them among themselves—two Sammy Sosas and one Randy Johnson for a Derek Jeter and a Mark McGwire. If you knew that your friend on the next block needed one particular player to complete his collection, and you had that player, the sky was the limit as to what you could demand.

Kids also flipped cards (heads or tails, odds or evens), tossed them against a wall or a stoop (closest one wins), stuck them between spokes on a bike (so they made a whirring sound), and carefully stored them in boxes that were kept in dresser drawers or closets. When baseball cards started to be worth real money, in the 1960s, lots of college students returning home on holiday break were heartbroken to discover that their mothers had thrown out the whole "worthless" collection with the trash. Like vintage comic books, old baseball cards in top condition can be worth hundreds or even thousands of dollars.

In the 1890s and the first couple of decades of the 1900s, sports cards came with packs of cigarettes. Mostly they pictured baseball players and boxers because those were the two most popular sports at the time. Professional football and hockey didn't really get started in this country until the 1920s and basketball not until even later. For example, the New York football Giants were born in 1925, the ice-hockey New York Rangers in 1926, and the basketball New York Knickerbockers in 1946. Compare that with the New York baseball Giants (1883) and the Yankees (1903).

Baseball cards in packs of bubble gum date from 1933, when the Goudey Gum Company of Boston first issued its Big League Chewing Gum cards, with a card and one slab of gum in a colorfully wax-wrapped 1-cent pack of bubble gum. The initial set of 239 cards cost $2.39 and included four cards of Babe Ruth and two of Lou Gehrig. The complete set in top condition was valued in 1998 at $48,000. The four Ruths alone fetch $19,000.

At the end of the thirties, Gum Incorporated of Philadelphia, which later became Bowman Gum, replaced Goudey as the leading producer of baseball cards. World War II interrupted the output of sports cards because of paper shortages, but in 1948 Bowman plunged back into business. That year's forty-eight cards cost 48 cents then and are now worth $3,500.

In 1951, Topps Chewing Gum Company of Brooklyn entered the field and gradually took over first place from Bowman. By the midfifties, Topps had bought out Bowman to become virtually the sole producer of baseball cards

The 1909 Honus Wagner, the six-hundred-pound gorilla of sports cards. In 1996, one was auctioned for $667,000.

until about 1980. In 1981, Donruss (of Memphis) and Fleer (based in Philadelphia) also started to issue bubble gum cards, breaking the virtual monopoly that Topps had held for twenty-five years. In the late eighties, Score and Upper Deck joined the three companies already producing sports cards, followed in the early nineties by subsidiaries called Leaf, Studio, Stadium Club, and Pinnacle.

What used to be a simple children's pastime has become a complicated and rather expensive adults' hobby. The bubble gum is long gone: New cards are now packaged by themselves, about ten in a pack that can cost between two and five dollars.

The value (price) of a previously issued card depends on supply and demand. The smaller the supply and the larger the demand, the higher the price. Supply is a simple matter of scarcity versus abundance. Demand is more complicated; it depends mainly on two things: (1) the player pictured on the card and (2) the card's physical condition.

Babe Ruth's 1933 card, considered a classic, is valued now at $5,000.

Home-run hitters and strike-out pitchers, for instance, are usually in greater demand than bench warmers or unsuccessful hurlers frequently knocked out of the pitcher's box. Similarly, the rookie card of a future star usually goes up in value when his career blossoms, while the rookie card of someone who gets sent back to the minors generally sinks with him. A rookie card, as its name implies, is a player's card in his first year in the major leagues—that is, when he is a rookie.

For several decades, the highest profile name in baseball cards, by far, has been Mickey Mantle.

His 1951 Bowman rookie card in top condition goes for $5,000, his 1952 Bowman for $2,000, his 1952 Topps for $17,000, and his 1953 Topps for $3,000. These figures easily surpass anyone else's cards in the same years.

Ken Griffey, Jr., and Mark McGwire are also hot. Junior's 1989 Upper Deck rookie card is valued at $90 (in contrast to the 1989 Upper Deck rookie card of second baseman Mark Lemke, for example, which is worth 10 cents).

With respect to physical condition, cards are classified on the basis of generally agreed-upon grading standards. The usual grades are as follows:

Mickey Mantle is the hottest name in sports cards. This 1953 Topps card brings $3,000.

- Mint Condition: A perfect card. Four sharp, square corners, with no creases, surface scratches, or fading.
- Near Mint: An *almost* perfect card. One with a very small defect, such as a very slight, almost imperceptible scratch.
- Excellent: Corners fairly sharp but showing moderate wear. Surface may show slight loss of luster from wear. But no creases.
- Very Good: Shows obvious handling. Corners rounded or minor creases.
- Good: A well-worn card, with rounded corners and/or major creases.
- Fair: Excessive wear, such as heavy creases or pencil marks.
- Poor: A card that has been run over by a tractor trailer.

As a general rule, the value of a card will fall by about half as it moves down each notch of the grading scale. If a Mint is worth $10, a Near Mint will sell for $5, an Excellent for $2.50, Very Good for $1.25, and so on. In fact, though, there isn't much of a market for newer cards rated below Excellent or for older cards rated below Very Good.

As the value of baseball and other sports cards has skyrocketed, the field has attracted counterfeiters. Modern color-printing technology makes counterfeiting quite feasible. The U.S. government has had to change the design and content of its twenty-, fifty-, and hundred-dollar bills to thwart counterfeiters, so it is not surprising that the sports card industry has faced similar problems. For that reason, many 1990s cards contain imprinted holograms (three-dimensional photographic images) that are intended to make counterfeiting more difficult.

Counterfeiting poses an even greater hazard for *autograph* collectors. Compared to counterfeiting cards, even the simplest ones, forging an autograph is a snap. It is easy to obtain examples of the autographs of most ballplayers, past as well as present, and after that it is just a matter of practice, practice, practice before they can be reproduced so it is hard for even an expert to distinguish a real signature from a forgery.

Autographs used to be inexpensive to obtain. Kids who lived in a city with a major league stadium would hang around the players' entrance and ask ballplayers to sign as they approached the ballpark. Other kids sent postcards or three-by-five index cards to players (there are books that give their mailing addresses), along with a stamped self-addressed envelope, and more often than not they got a response.

Now it's a whole different ballgame. Past and current players appear at widely promoted sports collectibles and card shows and sign their names—but only for cash. A charge of $30 to $50 for an autograph is not unusual, with prices escalating if the player is asked to sign anything out of the ordinary. For example, at a memorabilia and card show held in New Jersey in 1998, a sign next to Hall of Famer Willie McCovey stated that he would sign

Hank Aaron's rookie card, issued in 1954, is currently worth $1,500.

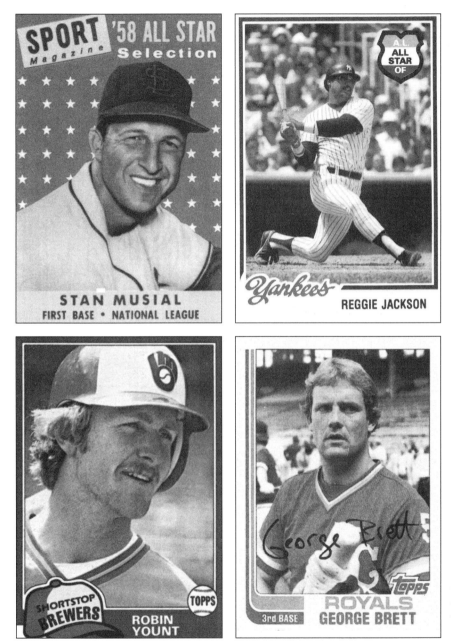

SPORT Magazine '58 ALL STAR Selection

STAN MUSIAL
FIRST BASE • NATIONAL LEAGUE

A.L. ALL STAR OF

Yankees
REGGIE JACKSON

SHORTSTOP BREWERS
ROBIN YOUNT
TOPPS

George Brett

ROYALS
3rd BASE GEORGE BRETT
Topps

Some typical
cards during
the period
1950 to 1989

flat items (such as photographs) or baseballs for $30, caps or equipment for $60, and bats or jerseys for $95.

Two of the best places still to obtain free autographs, and be sure they are genuine because they are signed right in front of you, are at spring training and at the Hall of Fame in Cooperstown, New York, on induction weekend. Players are more willing to sign during spring training than during the regular season. They are more approachable and more relaxed as well.

Each year the Baseball Hall of Fame holds induction ceremonies for newly elected Hall of Famers. Not only do the newly elected members attend but also many of the previously elected Hall of Famers. Probably on no other occasion can one obtain, in person, so many authentic quality autographs. Old-timers are generally more gracious about signing autographs than currently active players, and at Cooperstown few autograph-seekers are turned away.

Autograph values are determined by the same factors that determine card values—supply and demand. Supply is a matter of how many autographs someone signed. After a player dies, of course, the supply of his signature can no longer increase, assuming that forgeries don't add to the amount in existence.

Demand, as with cards, depends on *whose* autograph it is and its physical condition. Mickey Mantle, Joe DiMaggio, Ted Williams, and Babe Ruth are the Big Four. No matter how many autographs they sign, their signatures are always in demand. Baseballs autographed by Ted Williams or Joe DiMaggio are currently mass-marketed for $350 each. But Ken Griffey, Jr., and Mark McGwire are moving up rapidly.

With respect to physical condition, autographs can be in pencil or pen, faded or legible, on scraps of paper or on a photograph of the ballplayer, on a baseball or a bat or whatever. The more legible and long-lasting the signature, and the more attractive the object signed, the greater an autograph's value.

I used to think that ballplayers looked down on autograph collectors, thinking they were sort of childish. But a number of years ago

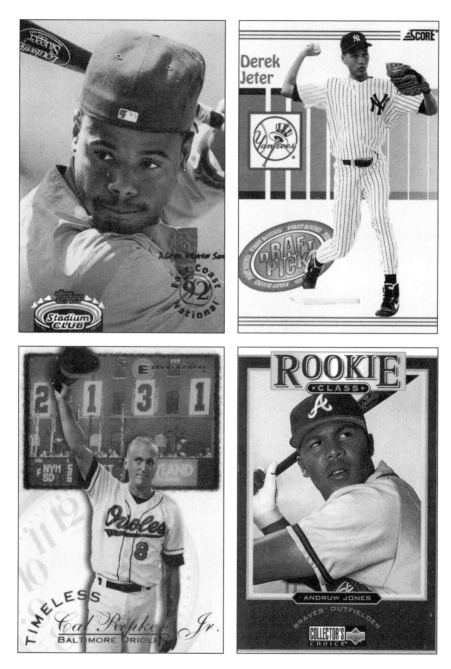

Typical baseball cards of the '90s

I did a book of reminiscences of old-time ballplayers, *The Glory of Their Times: The Story of the Early Days of Baseball Told by the Men Who Played It.* Many of the men in the book came to New York to attend a party celebrating its publication—Hall of Famers Rube Marquard, Sam Crawford, Stan Coveleski, Harry Hooper, Edd Roush, and Goose Goslin, as well as Chief Meyers, Fred Snodgrass, Lefty O'Doul, and a number of others. One afternoon I walked into the Warwick Hotel, where they were staying, and found all of them sitting around a large table, diligently signing and passing books from one to the other. Each was autographing his own chapter, signing his name next to his own photograph and making appropriate dedications to the others. It took hours, but they didn't mind because they obviously enjoyed giving and receiving autographs.

They formally presented one of the books to me, autographed by all of them. Its value is now estimated at $10,000—but it's not for sale!

Widely respected memorabilia collector Barry Halper tells a similar story. He recalls an incident at the New York Yankees' annual Old Timers' Day in 1980. All the Yankee living legends were on hand, from Joe DiMaggio to Mickey Mantle, Yogi Berra, and Whitey Ford, and all were besieged throughout the day for autographs.

Reggie Jackson, the Yankees' star right fielder at the time, expressed dismay at all the autograph-seekers. "I don't understand all this idolatry," Jackson told the assembled writers.

The next day, in the newspapers, there was a picture of Reggie Jackson handing a baseball to Joe DiMaggio and asking for his autograph!

*W*HY HAS BASEBALL REMAINED SO POPULAR FOR all these years? Since Alexander Cartwright first laid out the dimensions of the playing field and drew up the rules of the game, it has furnished enjoyment and excitement for countless millions of people, young and old alike.

Some believe the continued popularity of baseball is because it is a uniquely American game. But baseball is an important part of daily life not only in America but also in countries as diverse as Canada, Korea, Japan, Mexico, Venezuela, the Dominican Republic, and Cuba. Not to mention Puerto Rico, which is part of the United States but has its own cultural heritage.

If you think about it from a broader perspective, it isn't really Hank Aaron, with 755 lifetime home runs, who is the all-time home-run king. It's left-handed hitting Sadaharu Oh, first baseman of Tokyo's Yomiuri Giants, who hit his 756th home run on September 3, 1977. He retired in 1980, with 868 lifetime home runs. The son of a Chinese father and a Japanese mother, Oh is one of Japan's national heroes.

So it is not anything uniquely American about the game that accounts for its widespread and continued popularity.

Perhaps it is because baseball is a game that more or less "ordinary" people can play. Professional basketball players have to be very tall and football players very big. Many major league baseball players, however, are about six feet tall and weigh around 190 pounds, and some are much smaller.

For example, what do all of the following have in common:

Japan's Sadaharu Oh, the leading home run hitter of all time, became the manager of the Daiei Hawks.

Roberto Clemente, Len Dykstra, Jimmie Foxx, Rickey Henderson, Willie Mays, Mel Ott, Kirby Puckett, Pete Rose, and Honus Wagner? The answer is that all of them are less than six feet tall. And the list includes three men—Jimmie Foxx, Willie Mays, and Mel Ott—who each hit over five hundred career home runs.

Or perhaps it is freedom from the restraints of time that accounts for baseball's appeal. Time governs virtually everything we do in life, but it doesn't control baseball games. Baseball is the only team sport that dispenses completely with a clock. A ball game continues at its own pace for nine innings—more if necessary to determine a winner—regardless of how long it takes.

The fastest big league game ever played took only fifty-one minutes. The New York Giants beat the Philadelphia Phillies, 6–1, in that length of time on September 28, 1919.

By contrast, the longest major league game ever played took eight hours and six minutes, when the Chicago White Sox beat the Milwaukee Brewers, 7–6, in a game that went twenty-five innings on May 8 and 9, 1984. The game started on May 8 but wasn't completed until the next evening because play had to be suspended after seventeen innings, with the score tied, due to an American League curfew rule.

The longest game in major league history in terms of innings was a twenty-six-inning 1–1 tie between Brooklyn and Boston on May 1, 1920. The starting pitchers, Brooklyn's Leon Cadore and Boston's Joe Oeschger, both pitched the entire distance, the equivalent of almost three full games. The game took three hours and fifty minutes and was finally called on account of darkness at ten minutes to seven in the evening. If they had had lights back then, there's no telling how long they might have played.

An important factor that helps maintain interest in baseball from generation to generation is the huge statistical database that is continuously drawn upon by fans, reporters, announcers, managers, scouts, and even the players themselves. Babe Ruth hit sixty homers in 1927 and Phil Rizzuto only seven in 1950, when he was voted the American League's Most Valuable Player. Who played in the most consecutive games? Who hit safely in the most consecutive games? It is easy to find the answers to these and a million other baseball questions. No other sport has such a rich historical record about who did what when, from the very origins of the game in the mid-1800s right up to the present moment. Thus fans can compare Walter Johnson and Randy Johnson even though they pitched almost a century apart!

More likely than any of the above, however, in explaining the popularity of the game is the fluctuating drama in baseball that arises out of the succession of confrontations between two lonely people—the pitcher versus the batter. It is a contest of wits, intelligence, skill, and strength. It also involves more than a little courage because the ball is as hard as a rock and often comes toward home plate like a flash of lightning. And every so often it zooms in the opposite direction, over the fence for the game's most exciting hit—a home run!

The emotional tension ebbs and flows, with fairly long periods of apparent calm suddenly interrupted by bursts of action in which the game rides on every pitch.

A single, a stolen base, an error on an easy play, and all at once what had been a comfortable 4–1 lead no longer looks so safe. The pitcher starts to sweat, the batter feels the weight of responsibility on his shoulders, and the fielders move nervously back and forth smoothing the ground around their positions.

The crowd stops looking for a hot dog vendor and leans forward, rooting noisily or silently for one side or the other, anxiously awaiting the next pitch.

The suspense is heightened by the fact that most of the fans know each of the players as individuals. They have never met the players personally, but they know them better than they know their next-door neighbors—their backgrounds, their salaries, their family

Bob Feller pitching to Joe DiMaggio on April 30, 1946. How did DiMaggio do? Not
very well: Feller pitched a no-hitter that day.

problems, their physical and emotional ailments, whether they are easygoing or aggressive, their past successes and failures, and whether their careers are mostly behind or ahead of them.

Teams win or lose, but it is *individuals* who clearly and unmistakably bear the responsibility for victories or defeats. Baseball is a team game, but it is played by individuals who do their job singly and alone, in the full glare of the spotlight. They will be praised or blamed, become heroes or goats, depending on their performance under pressure.

That's how it was when Christy Mathewson faced Honus Wagner, when Sandy Koufax watched Hank Aaron walking up to the plate, when Roger Clemens looked down from the pitcher's mound and saw the menacing figure of Mark McGwire.

The confrontation between pitcher and batter is the same now as it was a hundred years ago. Human strengths and weaknesses are tested, and not only teams but also individual players and fans win or lose, depending on the outcome. Its appeal is evidently both universal and timeless.

Many of the photographs in this book are from The Card Memorabilia Associates in Peekskill, New York, and from the National Baseball Hall of Fame Library and Archive in Cooperstown, New York. I am deeply indebted to Michael P. Aronstein, President of TCMA, and to the pleasant and helpful people at the Baseball Hall of Fame, especially Patricia Kelly, W. C. Burdick, and John Horne, Jr., for their kind assistance.

I am equally grateful to Nat Andriani and Don Bowden, of Wide World Photos, for their friendly and generous help.

Aside from the photographs from TCMA and the Hall of Fame, the others are from the following sources:

Baltimore Orioles: 127
Robert C. Bartosz, Pennsauken, New Jersey: 58
Brown Brothers, Sterling, Pennsylvania: 15
Culver Pictures, New York: 14, 26, 121
Nancy Hogue, Warren, Ohio: 66 (bottom), 70 (top)
Richard Kavesh, Nyack, New York: 192
Ronald C. Modra, Port Washington, Wisconsin: 66 (top)
New York Daily News: 140
New-York Historical Society: 8
Photo File: 74, 78, 79, 83, 85, 90, 107, 116, 124, 125, 126, 133, 150, 161, 164
Louis Requena, Little Ferry, New Jersey: 138
TV Sports Mailbag: 94
United Press International: 38, 56, 61, 62, 70 (bottom), 111, 122, 142, 195
Wide World Photos: 44, 60

ABOUT THE AUTHOR

LAWRENCE S. RITTER is the author of *The Glory of Their Times: The Story of the Early Days of Baseball Told by the Men Who Played It*, which was called "one of the best baseball books ever published" by *The Sporting News* and was voted "all-time favorite baseball book" by readers of *The Sports Collectors Digest*. He is also coauthor of *Leagues Apart: The Men and Times of the Negro Baseball Leagues*, which was nominated for an NAACP Image Award, and of *The Babe: The Game That Ruth Built*, a pictorial biography of Babe Ruth. In addition, Mr. Ritter is a professor of finance and economics at New York University.